Writing & Thinking Skills:

SENTENCE WRITING

By Dorothy Rubin, Ph.D.
The College of New Jersey

Good Apple

A Division of Frank Schaffer Publications, Inc.

Editors: Lisa Schwimmer Marier, Christine Hood, Kristin Eclov
Book Design: RedLane Studio

 GOOD APPLE

A Division of Frank Schaffer Publications, Inc.
23740 Hawthorne Boulevard
Torrance, CA 90505-5927

GA13057

Contents

About This Resource

The ability to convey one's thoughts in writing is an essential skill, necessary for many aspects of our lives. Writing gives us a record of our thoughts, allowing us to stop to reflect, analyze, review, clarify, change, and understand better what we think. Learning about the writing process and how to write effectively is vital for all students.

Writing and Thinking Skills: Sentence Writing is a valuable resource for parents and teachers. This book contains a wealth of challenging, stimulating, and necessary writing and thinking skills and strategies for middle grade students. The wide variety of materials will help parents and teachers as they work with students of all ability levels. This excellent resource is published in a format that includes practice pages that are easily reproducible for distribution in classrooms or at home, as well as Student Study Pages with essential information your students can use as a guide in their writing.

Whom This Resource Is For

The materials in *Writing and Thinking Skills: Sentence Writing* are designed for students in approximately grades 5–8, but can be used with any students who need to improve their writing and thinking skills.

Recent national writing assessments have found that students appear to be gaining basic skills, though most still have difficulty demonstrating that they can apply these skills and use higher levels of thinking that involve analysis. This resource is aimed at the upper elementary grades because studies suggest that upper-elementary students are less likely to write on their own outside of school. *Writing and Thinking Skills: Sentence Writing* will ensure parents and teachers that their students are gaining the writing and thinking skills they need. This book will help improve students' test scores, including standardized achievement tests, as well as teacher-generated tests.

Organization

Within the introductory material, you will find information about each stage of the writing process, as well as two valuable checklists for both you and your students to use as references. A revision checklist is provided to ask questions concerning the creative improvement of the writing. The editing checklist asks questions concerning usage, sentence variety, capitalization, punctuation, and spelling. Use these lists as the basis to create your own checklist for your students to use as they write for different purposes.

The main body of this resource contains skill and strategy sections essential for students to write sentences effectively. Each skill and strategy section includes accompanying teaching material, learning objectives, special extension activities, Student Study Pages, and student practice sheets. The teaching material precedes the practices and contains the following:

Explanation
Modeling Strategy (not included for all skill areas)
Learning Objectives
Directions for Student Study Pages and Student Practices
Extensions

The extension activities are intended to extend learning in each of the skill areas. You may use some or all of these activities as appropriate for your students.

An Assessment Tool Progress Report appears at the end of the book (page 131). This report can be copied and used for each skill area. The Student Study Pages and student practice pages are also reproducible. The teaching material offers suggestions for record keeping and can be especially helpful for student portfolios.

Reproducible Student Study Pages are provided for students to use throughout the unit. Students can keep these pages available for reference as they work through the unit activities and when they do their own writing.

The student practices for each skill are graduated in levels of difficulty. You can choose appropriate practices based on the ability level of each student. Clear and understandable directions are provided for student practices.

Teaching Suggestions

Writing and Thinking Skills: Sentence Writing can be used in a number of ways. You can use the various pretests, revising, and editing checklists, as well as the diagnostic checklists that are provided at the end of this book to determine the needs of your students. Of course, you can use these sections in any order you feel is appropriate for your students.

The writing exercises in this book especially lend themselves to programs geared to helping students achieve more rigorous standards. The premise of this writing program is that most students can achieve at higher levels if they are provided with the proper teaching and help.

I encourage you to continuously assess your students' writing behavior. You can gain information about your students' writing using observation and student portfolios as well as, when appropriate, informal and formal diagnostic measures. You then can use this data to either reinforce, supplement, enrich, or develop skill and strategy areas.

You are the decision maker. You must determine, based on the developmental levels of your students, which concepts and the amount of instruction you need to provide.

The Writing Process

The writing process, which consists of a number of stages, refers to what we do when we are in the act of writing. That seems simple enough. However, when we attempt to analyze the writing process, we find that it is a complex thinking process analogous to problem solving.

Writing as a thinking act requires that we relate new information to our past experiences or existing information and that we analyze, synthesize, and evaluate this information so that we can present it in a coherent and logical manner. Writing as a thinking act requires time—time to mull over what we have written, dig deeper for greater understanding, create new ideas, destroy old ideas, explore our feelings, and evaluate as objectively as possible our creation.

When we acknowledge writing as a problem-solving process, we recognize that writing requires changes, rereading, rethinking, and rewriting. We understand that writing takes time, thinking, emotional involvement, and commitment to quality. The writing process consists of four major stages: *prewriting (or generating), drafting, revising,* and *editing.*

The **prewriting stage** consists of several steps before the actual writing. First, we begin with an area we would like to explore or write about. Next, we choose a topic and delimit it. Then, we must determine our audience (for whom we are writing). This will determine the design for our writing. After we have done this, we need to decide on our central theme, as well as our position on the subject. Next, we may need to discuss our views with someone or brainstorm some ideas, or we might want to do more research or reading about our topic.

Note that we have not yet begun the actual writing. Throughout our writing, we will continue to generate, analyze, organize, research, and recast our ideas.

We are now ready to begin writing. The **drafting stage** is when the writer puts down, in specific words, his or her ideas. As we already know, a good writer does not produce a finished, polished version at the first sitting or with the first draft.

In the **revising stage**, our writing is refined through thinking, writing, reading, critiquing, rewriting, rethinking, and so on; it concerns the creative improvement of the text. The writer makes changes, adds, deletes, reorganizes, and so forth, in order to say what he or she intends to say.

Finally, the writing reaches the **editing stage**, which focuses on the conventions of writing, including word choice and syntax, and the "fine tuning" of the work for a particular audience.

Special Note

Keep in mind that the writing of various drafts differs from the recopying of our writing. Some writers will go through a number of cycles of prewriting, drafting, and revising before they are satisfied that they have a draft to edit.

The Writing Process in Action

Prewriting Stage. Discuss the purpose of the writing assignment and who the students' audience will be. Brainstorm with students various topics they might like to write about. Help them choose a topic by modeling (thinking aloud) how you choose a topic. To choose their topics, students must keep in mind the audience for their writing, their knowledge of the topic, and the difficulty of the idea, as well as their own interest in the topic.

Do a mapping activity on a common topic students decide on, whereby you brainstorm words related to the topic. After the terms have been categorized and labeled, discuss them.

Next, have students gather information on the topic using various resource materials. Encourage them to discuss the information, analyze it, and finally decide on the point of view they want to take.

Drafting Stage. Now that students have decided on a topic, they can write their first drafts and so can you. Share with the class your first draft and explain your thoughts and ideas as you wrote. Explain how you tried to incorporate the central theme in your first paragraph and how you continually stopped to read and rethink what you wrote. Invite students to discuss what they did when they wrote their first drafts.

Revising Stage. Display your writing on an overhead projector so that students can see it. Then rewrite the draft "thinking out loud." Explain that when you reread what you had written, you realized that it did not say what you wanted, and it was not as clear as you thought it should be. You also realized that you did not have enough data to support your conclusions. Tell students that you need to do more research and reading on the topic. In addition, tell them that you are not correcting errors at this time, but rather concentrating on ideas presented in your paper. Explain that you will probably have to revise your writing a few times before it is the way you want it.

Ask students to revise their writing. Tell them you are available for individual help and discussion for anyone who wants or needs it. After students spend time on their revisions, discuss with them what they did and what kinds of changes they made.

Editing Stage. Again, place your writing on the overhead projector. Have students help you correct spelling, usage, and other errors. "Think out loud" about how you need to change some sentence structure to create more sentence variety and make your paper more interesting to read.

Then, ask students to edit their own work. When they're finished, have them compare their first drafts with their final ones. When the project is completed, display students' writing.

Special Note

The writing process applies to what we as individuals do when we are involved in writing. Not all of us proceed in the same way. Some students will spend a great deal of time thinking about what they will write before writing it, whereas others may commit pencil to paper almost immediately.

Be aware of these individual writing styles. Know when to intervene, how to intervene, and how much intervention an individual needs. Help students recognize when to "let go" of their writing, as well as when they should continue to revise and "polish."

Now, let's look a little more closely at a scenario of two student writers to see the writing process in action.

Scenario

Andrew and Kathy are fifth graders in Mrs. Smith's class. They are fortunate to have Mrs. Smith because she is a dynamic, enthusiastic teacher who is as knowledgeable of her students as of her subject. When you walk into Mrs. Smith's classroom, you sense immediately that this is a room where exciting learning is taking place. Conspicuously displayed is a whole shelf of children's bound books they have "published." Other books are also clearly visible, as well as several learning centers, children's art, and so on. What is most impressive to a visitor, however, is that when you walk into the classroom, no one notices you because each child is deeply immersed in what he or she is doing. The students in Mrs. Smith's class have been reading a number of fiction stories and books, and now they are going to write their own.

Prewriting Stage

Andrew has been interested in space travel for some time. As a matter of fact, his dream is to become an astronaut. There is almost no book on space travel in the school library that Andrew hasn't read, and the school librarian and Mrs. Smith have just ordered two new books for him "hot off the press." Andrew has no problem deciding what kind of fiction story he will write. It will be, of course, science fiction. Andrew is excited about his choice and discusses with Mrs. Smith some of his ideas. He also shares some of his thoughts with his friends. They, in turn, share some of their ideas with Andrew.

Kathy, however, is in a quandary because she can't decide on a topic. She hates to have to choose her own topic and isn't used to doing it. A transfer student from a school where the teachers always assigned the topic, Kathy has been in Mrs. Smith's class for only a few weeks. She will meet with Mrs. Smith for some help. Perhaps they can brainstorm some topics together.

Drafting Stage

Finally, Andrew decides that he has a good enough idea of the story he wants to write, so he decides to "give it a try." (This is not Andrew's first attempt at writing in Mrs. Smith's class—it's now the seventh month of the term, and students have been writing since the first day of class.) Andrew works for a concentrated period of time and seems oblivious to his surroundings. While he is working, no one interrupts him. Andrew only stops writing when the lunch bell rings. (Andrew surmises that it is about that time from the growls in his stomach.) Andrew is the kind of writer who likes to get everything down in his first draft.

Kathy, on the other hand, goes through her first draft very, very slowly because she doesn't like to keep revising and making new drafts. Kathy is more likely to think about and refine each sentence as she writes her first draft.

Andrew is so involved with his story that it is all he can talk about at lunch. If he has time during the day, he will try to get back to it. Kathy, however, says that she likes to mull things over. Anyway, there is something bothering her, and she doesn't know how to proceed. She discusses her problem with her friend Andrew, who makes a suggestion that she likes. She wants to think more about it, however.

By the next day, Andrew has finished his first draft. He worked on it at home because it was on his mind. Kathy does not complete her draft until the end of the week.

Revising Stage

Andrew rereads his first draft to himself rather than to Kathy, who is busy, because he is anxious to see how it holds together. He always likes to go over his material right away. Kathy, however, usually waits for a period of time before returning to her first draft. This gives her time to get away from her subject. Then she comes back to her work afresh. Andrew is reading his first draft to see whether he has to make any creative improvements to his story. In other words, he has to decide whether he needs to reorganize any of the material, and whether he needs to add, delete, or change anything. Because Andrew feels "stuck," he decides to meet with Mrs. Smith to discuss his story and ask for advice. Andrew does this, and, as usual, it pays off. Mrs. Smith listens carefully to what Andrew says. She takes her cues from him, and then asks some penetrating questions that help Andrew see his problems more clearly. (Before meeting with Mrs. Smith, Andrew knew what he had wasn't exactly what he wanted, but he had not been able to get at the problem.)

Andrew now knows what revisions to make; he sits down to write another draft. Actually, Andrew writes two more drafts before he is finally pleased with his story. He also meets two more times with Mrs. Smith to discuss his story.

Editing Stage

When Andrew finally feels he has the story exactly how he wants it, he goes over his paper to check whether he has made any usage, punctuation, capitalization, or spelling errors. (This is the part Andrew really dislikes.) Mrs. Smith wants the final copy to be as free from errors as possible. A paper or book filled with spelling, punctuation, and other errors is not one that people enjoy reading, even though the ideas are excellent.

Kathy and Mrs. Smith have worked together to edit her material. Because Kathy does most of her revising as she writes, it has taken her longer to work through her writing. Now, at the editing stage, Kathy checks for writing errors and then confirms with Mrs. Smith that she is happy with her finished product.

When Mrs. Smith reads Andrew's paper, she suggests that he might want to use some other words for variety, and she also picks up some spelling, capitalization, and punctuation errors. In addition, she makes some suggestions about sentence structure. After Andrew makes these corrections, Mrs. Smith asks him how he feels about his story and whether he feels it is ready for publication. Andrew claims that he is happy with it and wants it to be published.

Special Note

Publishing is one outcome of the writing process. If students are involved in publishing their own books, stories, or a group magazine, they will have a purpose for writing, revising, and editing. The amount of revision a student will do and the number of different drafts will depend on the student.

Revision and Editing Checklists

On the following pages, you will find two important checklists to use with your students' writing. The first, the Revision Checklist, concerns the creative improvement of the writing. The second, the Editing Checklist, concerns the final polishing of the writing. This second checklist is more extensive than the first. At the editing stage, the writer is concerned with having the most effective word choice and sentence structure to convey his or her message. The writer also wants text as free as possible from punctuation, capitalization, and spelling errors. Use these checklists as guides in working with students' writing, as well as to create your own checklist appropriate for your students. The amount of editing material listed on your group checklist depends on the individual differences of your students.

Revision Checklist

1. Does what you have written express what you want to say?

2. Should you add anything?

3. Should you delete some material?

4. Is your material well organized?

5. Is there a better way to organize your material?

6. Is there any new information or ideas that you feel you should incorporate in your writing?

7. Are you pleased with what you have written?

Name _____

Editing Checklist

1. Did you check your spelling and look up any words you are not sure of in the dictionary?

2. Do you have periods at the end of your sentences that should have periods?

3. Do you have question marks at the end of your sentences that ask a question?

4. Do you have capital letters at the beginning of all your sentences?

5. Do you have capital letters at the beginning of all names and names of things?

6. Did you capitalize the word *I* whenever you used it?

7. Did you put in commas where you are listing lots of things?

8. Did you put apostrophes in the proper places in making contractions such as *can't, don't, isn't, hasn't,* and *I'm*?

9. Did you use apostrophes in the correct places in writing possessives such as *Charles's, Joneses', enemies',* and *deer's*?

10. Did you check for agreement of subject and verb?

11. Did you check that your pronouns *(she, he, it)* agree with the correct subjects?

12. Did you use active voice whenever possible?

13. Did you avoid the overuse of dashes, brackets, or parentheses?

14. Did you check for run-on sentences?

15. Did you use the proper verb tenses?

16. Are your sentences complete sentences?

17. Did you avoid using sentences that are too wordy; that is, can you say the same thing in fewer words?

CAPITALIZATION

Explanation

A book on sentence writing cannot begin without a section on capitalization. Many students need extra practice learning what words should and should not be capitalized. Students may or may not have had previous experience with capitalization. During or by the end of the primary grade years, students should be able to capitalize words and phrases such as:

- proper names of people.
- the first word of a sentence.
- the greeting in a letter.
- the day and month of the year.
- titles of stories.
- titles preceding names, such as *Mrs., Mr., Ms., Miss,* and *Dr.*
- the first word of the closing of a letter, for example, *Yours truly, Sincerely yours, Your friend.*
- states, cities, streets, and avenues.
- the pronoun *I.*
- the first word of every line in a poem (with some exceptions).

During or by the end of eighth grade, students should be able to master all items of the previous years as well as capitalize:

- names of countries, towns, avenues, streets, and so on.
- any words used as a name, for example, *Mother* and *Father,* but not *his mother* or *her father.*
- titles of books, poems, stories, movies, and magazines, as well as names of languages, buildings, institutions, and companies.
- the first word of a direct quotation, historical periods, names of nationalities, or a direction that names a definite area.
- in outlining, the first word of each main topic, subtopic, and detail.

Modeling Strategy

Here is how one teacher models for her students the use of capitalization in her writing. Mrs. Gomez writes these sentences on the board:

> yesterday, jill and june left for st. louis. they will meet mr. gomez at sirs insurance company on second avenue.

Mrs. Gomez says, "I know that the first word in a sentence is always capitalized, so I will capitalize the *y* in the word *yesterday* in the first sentence and the *t* in the word *they* in the second sentence." Mrs. Gomez changes those letters to capital letters on the board. Then she says, "We learned that titles before names, such as *Mr.* or *Ms.* are capitalized, so I will make the title *Mr.* begin with a capital letter. I also know that names of people are capitalized. The names *Jill, June,* and *Gomez* should begin with capital letters.

Mrs. Gomez continues, "St. Louis is the name of a city, so that must be capitalized as well." Mrs. Gomez changes the letters so they are capital letters. "I'm almost done. We also learned that the names of companies and streets need capital letters. I will change these beginning letters and then read the sentence again to see if I missed anything."

Learning Objectives

Your students should be able to:

- Circle the words in each sentence that should be capitalized and correctly rewrite the sentence.
- Correct those sentences that are incorrectly capitalized and rewrite them correctly.
- Determine whether an item is correctly capitalized or not.
- Construct sentences using correct capitalization.

Directions for Student Study Pages and Practices

Use the student pages (pages 20–28) to help your students acquire, reinforce, and review capitalization. They can begin with the activity on page 20 as a review of what they know about capitalization. Encourage students to check their own answers as well as assess their progress with the Student Progress Assessment Record on page 21. Reproduce the Student Study Pages on pages 22 and 23 for each student. They can be used as references while students do the practices, as well as when they do their own writing.

Pick and choose the practices based on the needs and developmental levels of your students. Answers for the student review and practice pages are reproducible, so you may choose to give your students the practice pages, as well as the answer pages, to progress on their own. The answers are on pages 145 and 146.

Extensions

■ Provide sheets of rectangular stickers for students to create address cards for themselves and their families. Or, you can provide smaller stickers to make return address stickers for students and their families to use when mailing letters and cards. Students can use pens or markers to write their names and addresses on each sticker, adding illustrations if they like.

■ Ask students to think of funny titles for stories, songs, and books they would like to see, such as:

Books:	*Teachers Who Have Gone Wrong*
	How to Skip High School Completely
Songs:	"School's Out Forever"
	"You Think You're So Cool, But You're Not"

Invite students to write their titles on the board using correct capitalization. Have students vote on the funniest, most creative, and most interesting titles.

Name _____

Student Review for Capitalization

Directions: Rewrite the following sentences using capital letters correctly.

1. mr. and mrs. j. s. hill are the parents of eric and ilse.

   _____

   _____

2. in may, my Brother and i are going to School in a small Town in texas.

   _____

   _____

3. in the Summer, my Parents and i are going to visit the smithsonian institution in washington, d.c.

   _____

   _____

4. kelsey, melissa, anna, and i are going to a party at the perez's house on warren street in october.

   _____

   _____

5. my Cousin, my Sister, my Aunt, and i will visit new york city the last monday in june.

   _____

   _____

Capitalization Review

Student Progress Assessment Record

Count how many items you answered correctly in the Student Review for Capitalization. Write your score in the *My Score* column. Look at the score in the *Good Score* column. If your score is as high as the good score, you are ready to continue with the next skill. If your score falls below the good score, review the information related to Capitalization to make sure you have learned the material. Then move on to the next skill.

Capital Letters	Good Score	My Score	Review Pages
Sentence 1	6–7		
Sentence 2	6–7		
Sentence 3	8–9		
Sentence 4	8–9		
Sentence 5	9–10		

Student Study Pages

Capitalization

In order to be a good writer, you need to know what words should be capitalized. Here is a list of items that should be capitalized:

The first word of a sentence	My friend is not going to the party.
Names of persons	Sharon Johnson, Carol Smith
Titles of persons	Mr., Mrs., Ms., Dr., Reverend, Captain
Days of the week	Sunday, Monday, Tuesday, Wednesday
Months of the year	January, February, March, April
Titles of books	*Twenty Thousand Leagues Under the Sea*
Titles of plays	*A Christmas Carol*
Titles of magazines	*Cricket, Mad*
Titles of poems	"Fog," "Eletelephony"
Titles of movies	*The Wizard of Oz*
Titles of stories	"The Monkey's Paw"
Names of countries	the United States of America, France, England
Names of cities	San Francisco, Miami, New York, Minneapolis
Names of streets, avenues, and roads	Tenth Street, Stuart Road, Fifth Avenue
Names of languages	Chinese, Spanish, Italian, English, Japanese
Names of companies	Autodynamics Inc., IBM, Jackson Trade Co.
Names of institutions	Ford Foundation
Historical periods	the Stone Age, the Prehistoric Age
Names of wars	World War II, the Korean War
Documents	the Declaration of Independence
Buildings	the Empire State Building
The pronoun *I*	It was only Josh and I who went to the party.

Student Study Pages *continued*

The first word of every line in poetry (with some exceptions)

Whose woods these are I think I know
His house is in the village though;

Names of God

Lord, Father, He (and pronouns used for God)

The first word of a direct quotation

Jennifer said, "That is a scary ride."

Do *not* capitalize the following:

Seasons

summer, fall, winter, spring

Games

football, chess, tennis

School subjects (unless they are names of languages)

math, geography, history, English, French

Names of relatives (unless they are used as part of the person's name)

mother, father, sister, Aunt Mary, Uncle John, Dad

A direction (unless it names a definite area or is part of a name)

east, west, north, south, southeast, North America, South Dakota
We live in the East. They went east.

Words used in a general sense (rather than as a name or part of a title)

captain, hospital, avenue, bank, general

Special Note

All words in titles are capitalized except for small words such as *a, an, and, the, of, from,* and *to,* which are *not* capitalized in a title unless they begin the title. (All verbs in titles, including short verbs, such as *Is, Am,* and *Be,* are capitalized.)

Name_____

Practice 1

Directions: Here are ten sentences. Circle the word or words in each sentence that should be capitalized. Then rewrite the sentence correctly.

1. my aunt sally came to visit us from europe.

   _____

2. i do not do well in english.

   _____

3. ms. amad lives on seventh avenue in minneapolis.

   _____

4. our uncle lives in the south, and our grandparents live in the west.

   _____

5. in our history class, we are studying the constitution of the united states.

   _____

6. no one knew that mr. brown wrote the poem "life's moments."

   _____

7. on sunday, our school is having a picnic in the new part of town.

   _____

8. the football game was held in davis stadium on saturday.

   _____

9. ricardo, sandy, chuck, and nate received a special award in january.

   _____

10. rashid said, "not even alisa and i are going on monday."

   _____

24

Name _____

Practice 2

Directions: Here are ten sentences. Each sentence contains words that are capitalized incorrectly. Circle the words that should not be capitalized. Then rewrite the sentence with correct capitalization.

1. My Father, Mother, and uncle Dave got lost on Tuesday in an old part of Town.

   _____

2. I enjoy History, Geography, and Languages such as German and French.

   _____

3. On Sunday we usually go skating in the Park, and then we go to a Restaurant to eat.

   _____

4. Football and Basketball are my favorite sports, but I'm better in Chess than in either of the others.

   _____

5. When my Cousin fell, we took him to the Hospital.

   _____

6. In the Summer, I usually go to Camp with my Brother.

   _____

7. When we traveled North last Spring, I met a famous Poet.

   _____

8. In the Olden Days, children used to recite verse, such as the following: "I was ever born in Sin,/And all my Heart is bad within."

   _____

9. I enjoyed my trip West, but I was surprised that I did not see many Actresses and Actors in Hollywood.

   _____

10. The Stewards on the Ship told all the Passengers to be calm, but it's difficult to be calm with hurricane Diane raging over you.

    _____

Name _____

Practice 3

Directions: Here are five sentences. Each sentence contains words that are capitalized incorrectly. Rewrite each sentence with correct capitalization.

1. my Father is a Doctor, and my Mother is a Lawyer.

   _____

   _____

2. the Title of my Poem is "the Trials Of A bug."

   _____

   _____

3. Spring and Fall are the seasons i like the best.

   _____

   _____

4. when rev. Jim brown spoke, everyone in the Audience listened.

   _____

   _____

5. my favorite Aunt is aunt Jane, and my favorite Uncle is Uncle Peter.

   _____

   _____

Name _____

Practice 4

Directions: Here is a list of items. If the item is correctly capitalized, write a *C* in the blank. If the item is not correctly capitalized, rewrite it correctly.

1. chrysler building _____

2. *the Taming Of The Shrew* _____

3. Winter _____

4. ms. Smith _____

5. "The Hare and the Tortoise" _____

6. General Grant _____

7. dr. Sarah brown _____

8. social studies _____

9. wednesday _____

10. the Renaissance _____

11. i _____

12. the joneses _____

13. a Map _____

14. Georgia _____

15. egypt _____

16. asia _____

17. Blanding street _____

18. aunt Sharon _____

19. Cousin _____

20. *the Boy who Could make Himself Disappear* _____

_____

Name _____

Practice 5

Directions: Follow the instructions in parentheses.

1. (Write a sentence that contains the names of two people and the name of a city.)

   _____

   _____

2. (Write a sentence that contains a person with a title, a month of the year, and a day of the week.)

   _____

   _____

3. (Write a sentence that contains the title of a book.)

   _____

   _____

4. (Write a sentence that contains two of your favorite school subjects and games.)

   _____

   _____

5. (Write a sentence that contains the title of one of your favorite poems.)

   _____

   _____

PUNCTUATION

Explanation

When you speak, your voice, your face, and your body movements help give meaning to what you are saying. When you write, **punctuation marks** are the signals that help readers understand your meaning. Here are the punctuation signals that are used to replace the stress, pitch, and pauses you use when you speak.

. period
, comma
; semicolon
: colon
? question mark
__ underline
! exclamation point
— dash
( ) parentheses
[ ] brackets
" " quotation marks

In this book, students are presented with exercises dealing with the following:

. period
? question mark
! exclamation point
, comma
; semicolon
" " quotation marks

This section on punctuation should reinforce some of the material presented later in the book and help students learn some of these needed punctuation skills.

During or by the end of the primary grade years, students should be able to place:

- periods at the end of sentences.
- periods after abbreviations such as *Ave., St.,* and *Dr.*

- question marks at the end of question sentences.
- exclamation points at the end of sentences that express great emotion.
- commas within dates, for example, *February 11, 2010.*
- commas in addresses, for example, *East Orange, New Jersey 07017;* or *Los Angeles, California 90040.*
- commas after greetings in friendly letters, such as *Dear Sara,.*
- commas after closings in letters, such as *Yours truly,* and *Sincerely,.*
- periods after numbers in lists, for example, *1. 2. 3. 4. 5.*
- periods after *Mr., Mrs.,* and *Ms.*
- periods after initials, for example, *S. A. Johnson.*
- apostrophes in some contractions such as *can't* or *she's.*
- apostrophes in singular possessives such as *girl's* or *boy's.*

During or by the end of eighth grade, students should be able to master all items of the previous years as well as using:

- apostrophes in more contractions.
- apostrophes in singular and plural possessives, for example, *John's, Ian's,* and *Maria's;* as well as *the students' homework* or *the Joneses' home.*
- hyphens between syllables when separating words at the end of lines.
- exclamation points for command sentences only if the command expresses great emotion, for example, *Help, help!*
- commas to separate items in a series, such as *milk, butter, eggs,* and *cheese.*
- colons after salutations in business letters, for example, *Dear Sir:*
- commas to set off quotations, for example, *Frank said, "Hello."*
- quotation marks before and after quotations, for example, *Frank said, "I can't go."*
- commas in numbers containing four or more digits, as in *1,000* or *12,965* (optional for four-digit numbers).
- commas with transitional words such as *however, indeed, nevertheless, that is, for example, in fact,* and *so on.*
- quotation marks for special words in sentences, for example, *She had a "pained" look on her face.*
- quotation marks to set off titles of poems, short stories, magazine articles, chapters, and so on, for example, the poem "The Monkey's Paw."
- colons to set off lists of items, for example, *They had the following at the bake sale: cakes, cookies, bread, bread sticks, pies, and tarts.*
- underlining for book titles such as <u>War and Peace</u> and <u>Gone with the Wind</u>.

Special Note

Please note that the sections dealing with "Complex Sentences" (page 89) and "Sentence Expansion Using Modifiers" (page 112) have important information concerning the use of commas with restrictive and nonrestrictive modifiers. This punctuation area is being presented as background information because it is confusing for many writers.

Modeling Strategy

Here is how one teacher models for her students how to use punctuation to give meaning to sentences. The teacher tells the students that they have been reviewing many punctuation skills and today she will present them with more punctuation skills to help them in their writing. She says, "Punctuation marks are signals. They help give meaning to what you are writing. When driving a car, a red light tells us to stop and a green light tells us to go. When we speak, we use hand movements, facial expressions, and our voices to help others get the meaning of what we are saying. We use punctuation in the same way—to express better what we mean in our writing. I will write one sentence on the board. Then I will say aloud what goes through my mind as I analyze the sentence on the board. You will see how the meaning of the sentence changes based on the punctuation I use." The teacher writes the following on the board.

1) Go home now.

2) Go home now?

3) Go home now!

Then she says, "Let me see. The first sentence could be a statement or a command. It's not a very strong command because there isn't any exclamation point at the end. I guess someone is just telling me to go home at this time. The second sentence is a question whether I should go home now. There seems to be doubt about doing this. The third sentence, on the other hand, is quite insistent that I should go home now. The last sentence is an urgent command.

"Remember, you do not use an exclamation point unless you want to express some kind of urgency. Be wary about using exclamation points too much."

Learning Objectives

Your students should be able to:

- Correctly punctuate the end of given sentences.
- Construct and correctly punctuate the end of sentences.
- Correctly insert commas in given sentences.
- Use commas to shorten sentences.
- Correctly insert a comma or a semicolon or both in given sentences.
- Insert quotation marks in those sentences that need them.
- Change sentences with indirect quotations into sentences with direct quotations.

Directions for Student Study Pages and Practices

Use the student pages (pages 34–46) to help students acquire, reinforce, and review punctuation. They can begin with the activity on page 34 as a review of what they know about punctuation. Encourage students to check their own answers as well as assess their progress with the Student Progress Assessment Record on page 35. Reproduce Student Study Pages on pages 36–39 for each student. This section can be used for reference while students do the practices, as well as when they do their own writing.

Pick and choose the practices based on the needs and developmental levels of your students. Answers for the student review and practice pages are reproducible, so you may choose to give your students the practice pages, as well as the answer pages, to progress on their own. The answers are on pages 146–148.

Extensions

■ Invite students to create sentences on the board using various punctuation marks. Then invite other students to come to the board and change the sentences by using different punctuation. Have students note how the sentence meanings change with different punctuation. For example:

I have to leave now.	I have to leave now?
Don't go there.	Don't go there!
Carol Sweeti and Bill went to the movies.	Carol, Sweeti, and Bill went to the movies.

■ Challenge students to read paragraphs from books using all exclamation points or all question marks. Invite students to write out the paragraphs and change all of the punctuation to make changes in the meaning of the paragraphs. Share the paragraphs with the rest of the group.

Name _____

Student Review for Punctuation

Directions: Follow the directions for each of the following sections.

1. Shorten the following phrases into contractions.

   a. could not _____   f. they are _____

   b. will not _____   g. I am _____

   c. did not _____   h. she will _____

   d. can not _____   i. we are _____

   e. he is _____   j. it is _____

2. Punctuate the following correctly.

   a. Dear Rasheen   g. Mr

   b. Sincerely yours   h. Mrs

   c. How old are you   i. Help

   d. I am eleven years old   j. Ave

   e. Ms   k. C A Smith

   f. Dr   l. S Jones

3. Write the following singular nouns as possessives.

   a. man _____   f. apple _____

   b. girl _____   g. lady _____

   c. book _____   h. boy _____

   d. class _____   i. Dallas _____

   e. student _____   j. watch _____

4. Rewrite the following with correct punctuation.

   a. april 1 1999 _____   d. j j jackson _____

   b. john st _____   e. k s perry _____

      trenton new jersey 08625   73 cherry ave _____

      _____   manhasset hills new york 11040

   c. may 25 1952 _____   _____

Punctuation Review

Student Progress Assessment Record

Count how many items you answered correctly in the Student Review for Punctuation. Write your score in the *My Score* column. Look at the score in the *Good Score* column. If your score is as high as the good score, you are ready to continue with the next skill. If your score falls below the good score, review the information related to punctuation to make sure you have learned the material. Then move on to the next skill.

Punctuation	Good Score	My Score	Review Pages
Contractions	9–10		
Punctuation Marks (general)	6–7		
Possessives	9–10		
Punctuation Marks & Capitalization	23–26		

Student Study Pages

Punctuation

When you speak, your voice, your facial expressions, and your body movements help give meaning to what you are saying. **Punctuation marks** are the "signals" that help give meaning to what you write. Here are the punctuation marks that you will be working with in the following punctuation practices.

.	**period**
?	**question mark**
!	**exclamation point**
,	**comma**
;	**semicolon**
" "	**quotation marks**

Punctuating the Ends of Sentences

Punctuation marks help the reader know whether a sentence is a statement, question, command, or sentence of strong feeling. For example:

Jennifer is a pretty girl.

This is a declarative (statement) sentence. It is the most often written sentence. A **period** (.) is placed at the end of this kind of sentence.

Who did that?

This is an interrogative (question) sentence. A **question mark** (?) ends this kind of sentence.

I love it!

This sentence is an exclamatory sentence—one that expresses strong feeling. An **exclamation point** (!) ends this kind of sentence.

Stop that.

This is an imperative sentence—it expresses a command. A period is most often used to end this kind of sentence; however, an exclamation point may be used to show strong feeling. The subject in a command sentence is usually understood; that is, it is usually not stated. The sentence *Stop that* really says *You stop that.*

Student Study Pages *continued*

Special Note

An interjection, which is considered a part of speech, is a word usually used with an exclamation point to express strong feeling. An interjection is independent of the rest of the sentence. For example:

Oh!

Hurrah!

Goodness!

The Comma

The **comma** (,) is the most often used punctuation mark. The comma, like other punctuation marks, is a signal that helps readers better understand a written message. A comma signals a pause. This pause is not as strong as the stop signaled by a period (.). The comma is used

to shorten sentences

Sharon jogs and Seth jogs and Jennifer jogs.
Sharon, Seth, and Jennifer jog.

We played basketball and tennis and chess.
We played basketball, tennis, and chess.

Arthur is kind and smart and friendly.
Arthur is kind, smart, and friendly.

In these sentences, the comma is used to replace the word *and* in a series—a group of three or more items or events.

in compound sentences

My mother is a lawyer, and my father is an engineer.
I plan to be a skydiver, and my brother intends to be a pilot.
My friends waste a lot of time after school, but I don't.

In these sentences, a comma is used to separate simple sentences joined by such conjunctions as *and, but, for, or, nor,* and *yet.*

Student Study Pages *continued*

after a dependent clause

When Steve arrived at the party, it was time to go home.
Although he is my best friend, he sometimes gets on my nerves.

In these sentences, a comma is used after a **dependent clause**—a group of words that cannot stand alone as a sentence—when it comes before an independent clause, which is a group of words that can stand alone as a sentence.

Usually commas are not placed before descriptive words that refer to size, color, or age. For example:

She is a nice little old lady.
I have a pretty red hat.

The Semicolon

The **semicolon** (;) is a stronger punctuation signal than the comma. When linking words, such as *also, therefore, so, moreover, however, then,* and *nevertheless,* join two simple sentences to form a compound sentence, a semicolon is usually used before the linking word. For example:

Dick is an excellent musician; however, he doesn't like to practice.
We waited for the team to arrive; then we cheered and applauded them.
I need a lot of energy to play football; therefore I eat a lot.

Special Note

Either a comma or a semicolon may be used with the linking word *so.*

Quotation Marks

Quotation marks (" ") are always used when you write

a direct quotation

Emma said, "I will not be home for dinner."
Sarah said, "I do not have enough money to buy lunch."
Art asked, "What time is it?"
Laura replied, "I don't know."

In a direct quotation, put a comma after the word *said* and capitalize the first word of the quotation. A **direct quotation** gives a statement in the exact words of a speaker.

Student Study Pages *continued*

Special Note

Notice that the period and the question mark are placed *inside* the quotation marks for the above sentences.

---

titles of poems, songs, stories, articles, and chapters

"Fog"
"America the Beautiful"
"The World's Urban Areas"

Titles of this kind are enclosed in quotation marks.

Quotation marks (" ") are *not* used when you write

an indirect quotation

She said that she wasn't sure about two of her answers.
He asked whether we were going to the party.
We replied that we didn't know.

An **indirect quotation** does not give the exact words. It merely gives an approximation of what was or might have been said. An indirect quotation is not enclosed in quotation marks.

Name_____

Practice 1

Directions: Here are ten sentences without punctuation marks. Write each sentence with the correct punctuation mark at the end of it.

1. Who are you _____

   _____

2. Don't go yet _____

   _____

3. I need more time to do that _____

   _____

4. When are you leaving _____

   _____

5. That is fantastic _____

   _____

6. We all passed our exams _____

   _____

7. Henry refused to go to the party with us _____

   _____

8. Imagine that _____

   _____

9. Stop _____

   _____

10. Is he telling the truth _____

    _____

40

Name _____

Practice 2

Directions: Follow the instructions in parentheses.

1. (Write a question sentence.)

_____

_____

2. (Write a statement sentence.)

_____

_____

3. (Write a command sentence.)

_____

_____

4. (Write a sentence that expresses strong feeling.)

_____

_____

5. (Write a command sentence that expresses strong feeling.)

_____

_____

Name_____

Practice 3

Directions: Insert commas where needed in the following sentences. If a sentence does not need a comma, write the letter *O* in the blank. **Hint:** If you are unsure about adding a comma in a series of words that describes another word, check to see if the word *and* can replace the comma. If it can, you should use a comma.

_____ 1. My pretty little sister is crying.

_____ 2. The little old lady walked down the street.

_____ 3. Jack Alicia and Marta are not here.

_____ 4. Jim went swimming before breakfast before lunch and before dinner.

_____ 5. My favorite subjects are French English and geography.

_____ 6. Kayla is smart pretty and fun to be with.

_____ 7. My best friend is a member of the chorus a member of the band and a member of the debate club.

_____ 8. He is poor tired and sad.

_____ 9. The big black dog bit me.

_____ 10. The bell rang once twice and three times.

Name _____

Practice 4

Directions: Insert commas where needed in the following sentences. If a sentence does not need a comma, write the letter *O* in the blank.

_____ 1. My friend is good and kind.

_____ 2. The bell rang very loudly and then the children stopped playing.

_____ 3. I studied hard for the exam but the material I studied wasn't on it.

_____ 4. My friend passed the exam for she had studied the correct material.

_____ 5. I passed the exam but I did not get a good grade on it.

_____ 6. Yesterday I studied for the wrong exam and I had an argument with my friend.

_____ 7. The ride was scary thrilling and breathtaking.

_____ 8. I tried out for the football team and my friend tried out for the basketball team.

_____ 9. The guys on the football team are strong big and athletic.

_____ 10. Our uniforms are green white and yellow.

_____ 11. After Jim left the room people began to say mean things about him.

_____ 12. I dislike people who make fun of others.

_____ 13. When my best friend started to poke fun at Jim I became very upset.

_____ 14. Jill Josh Elise and I left the party and went home.

_____ 15. When my big black dog greeted me at the door I felt good.

Name_____

Practice 5

Directions: Shorten the following sentences using commas. Write your shortened sentences in the spaces provided.

1. My brother and my sister and my father and my mother are coming to visit my class.

   _____

   _____

2. I enjoy playing games and I enjoy watching television and I enjoy reading.

   _____

   _____

3. Yesterday we swam and we water-skied and we hiked.

   _____

   _____

4. The cat is cute and cuddly and smart.

   _____

   _____

5. My friend Tyrel and my friend Jim and my friend Jack are studying for a history test and a math test and an English test.

   _____

   _____

6. My favorite flavors are vanilla and chocolate and strawberry.

   _____

   _____

44

Name _____

Practice 6

Directions: Insert a comma or semicolon or both in the following sentences.

1. The train arrived two hours late for it had engine trouble.

2. When my parents changed jobs we had to move to another state.

3. Even though my brother is a star athlete he is not a snob.

4. I never get away with anything however my sister always does.

5. My sister is a cheerleader therefore she gets to go to all the games.

6. I have to be home by a certain time but my sister can stay out as late as she wants.

7. Art is my favorite subject but I am a terrible artist.

8. The door opened slowly then a huge hand came into view and turned out the lights.

9. After I saw my mistakes I felt ill.

10. If I don't do better on the next exam I won't be able to play in the big game.

Name_____

Practice 7

Directions: Insert quotation marks where needed in the following sentences. If a sentence does not need quotation marks, write the letter O in the blank.

_____ 1. He said that he was not playing in the game.

_____ 2. Our class decided to recite poems such as Chicago, Birches, and The Sea for our parents.

_____ 3. After reading the chapter Controlled Experiments in the Classroom, we ran our own controlled experiments.

_____ 4. Britta said, I learned some interesting things from my controlled experiment.

_____ 5. Our teacher said that he also learned some interesting things from our experiments.

Directions: Change each sentence with indirect quotations into a sentence with direct quotations. Write the sentence in the space below.

Examples: John said that he couldn't answer the question.

John said, "I can't answer the question."

6. Marika said that she needed more paper.

_____

_____

7. Jake asked why they were not going on the plane yet.

_____

_____

8. Ben said that the plane was delayed because of a storm.

_____

_____

9. Our instructor asked whether we understood the question.

_____

_____

WRITING SIMPLE SENTENCES

Explanation

The **sentence** is a significant unit of language, a unit of meaning. It is a word or group of words stating, asking, commanding, supposing, or exclaiming. A sentence contains a subject and a verb that are in agreement with one another. It begins with a capital letter and ends with a period (.), question mark (?), or exclamation point (!). There are four types of sentences: *simple, compound, complex,* and *compound-complex.*

There are clear-cut rules for correct sentences, but correct style is a much more complicated matter. Short sentences are used for effect, and so are longer sentences. There are times for repetition in writing, and there are times for brevity. Good writers use word imagery and descriptive phrases to make their writing colorful and interesting. Knowledge of how to use various methods of expanding and combining sentences, as well as how to avoid using "overworked phrases," helps develop writing style.

Special Note

Exercises on recognizing simple, compound, complex, and compound-complex sentences are presented in the student practice pages. However, the emphasis is on *writing* sentences. The recognition practices are presented to make students aware of the different types of sentences that they encounter in their everyday reading and to help them gain experience in working with them.

Simple Sentences

A **simple sentence:**

■ contains a word or group of words that names something (subject) and says something about the thing named (predicate). It expresses a complete meaning or thought.

Jack is happy.

- consists of one single statement, command, wish, question, or exclamation.

> Larry is playing the violin.
> Stay here.
> Who is he?
> She is a beautiful baby!

- may be as brief as one word if it expresses a complete thought. In each of the following sentences the subject, *you,* is understood. The punctuation helps give meaning.

> Run.
> Wait.
> Help!

- may have a single subject (noun or pronoun) and a single or compound verb or a compound subject (two or more) and a single or compound verb.

> Debbie jogs every morning.
> George and Debbie jog every morning.
> Franchesca jogs and swims every morning.
> Laura and Franchesca jog and swim every morning.

- contains only one independent clause. An **independent clause** is a group of words that contains both a subject (noun or pronoun) and a predicate (verb). An independent clause can stand alone as a sentence because it "makes sense" by itself.

Special Note

Sentence fragments (incomplete parts) cannot stand alone as sentences. Sentence fragments such as *Around the corner, Into the lake, When they arrive,* and *Among the six of us* are not sentences. Although the group of words *When they arrive* has a subject and a predicate, it cannot stand alone as a sentence because the thought signaled by the word *when* has not been completed.

During or by the end of the primary grade years, students are able to write many different kinds of simple sentences. They can write simple sentences containing:

- a single subject and single verb: *Rashid swims.*
- a single subject and compound (two or more) verb: *Rashid runs and swims.*
- a compound subject and single verb: *Rashid and Tonya swim.*
- a compound subject and compound verb: *Rashid and Tonya run and swim.*

During or by the end of the intermediate grade years, students are able to:

- recognize that a sentence is a group of words stating, asking, commanding, supposing, or exclaiming.
- recognize that a sentence contains a subject and verb that are in agreement in number with one another.
- write a simple sentence with a compound subject and a compound verb.
- recognize that a simple sentence has one group of words that can stand alone as a simple sentence because it has a subject and verb that expresses a complete thought.
- recognize that a simple sentence may be as brief as one word. For example: *Stop. Go. Help!*
- recognize that in sentences such as the preceding, the subject *you* is understood and the punctuation helps give meaning to the sentence.
- recognize that sentence fragments such as *Into the store, When she came, Along the way, And in a second,* and *Although he is* are not sentences.
- recognize that sentences must have correct word order to make sense.

Modeling Strategy

Here is how one teacher models for his students how to write better sentences. The teacher tells the students that they have been writing for a long time, so they already know many things about sentences. Now they will be learning more about them, so they can become really good writers. He then says, "In order to help you learn about sentence order and that sentences must express a complete thought, I will say aloud exactly how I figure these things out."

The teacher tells the students that sentences must make sense. That means that sentences must have a certain word order. He writes the following sentences on the board. Then he says, "Let me show you what I mean. Here are two groups of words:

Gregory rollerbladed very fast down the hill.
Gregory hill the fast very rollerbladed down.

"Let me read both groups of words aloud. The first group of words makes sense. The second group, however, doesn't. The words are all mixed up. In order for a sentence to make sense, the words must be in correct order." The teacher gives the students some practices, such as the following, to make sure they understand the concept he presented.

Bethany in park skating the went.
Earl rode his bike in town.
Pat fast is.

The teacher then tells the students that sentences must express a complete thought. He writes the following groups of words on the board:

1. Rollerblading in the park.
2. Skating here.
3. Melissa and Kelsey are in school. ✓
4. Ben and Oliver run very fast. ✓
5. While in the park.
6. Go. ✓
7. Help! ✓
8. Please stay here with me. ✓

The teacher then says, "It seems to me that sentence one isn't a sentence because it doesn't tell me who is rollerblading in the park, so it must be a sentence part or fragment. The same is true for sentence two. I don't know who is skating here. When I look at sentences six and seven, however, I notice that even though there is only one word in both sentences, they each express a complete thought. The word *you* is understood. In other words, even though it's not stated, each sentence says, 'You go; you help.' The same is true for sentence eight. The sentence says, 'You please stay here with me.' Sentences three and four are sentences because they each express a complete thought. Sentence five is only a sentence part because it doesn't express a complete thought. The words *While in the park* don't tell me anything about what happened while in the park or to whom or what something happened while in the park."

To make sure students understand the concept he presents, the teacher gives them groups of words, such as the following, and asks them to draw a line under those that are complete sentences. After they have finished the activity, the teacher goes over each group of words and gives students the results.

1. <u>Please go to the board.</u>
2. Tony and I.
3. <u>We are going to the movies.</u>
4. <u>Is that real?</u>
5. When she stays.
6. While in school.
7. <u>Stay away from there.</u>
8. <u>Help.</u>
9. <u>Don't go.</u>
10. Into the park.

WRITING SIMPLE SENTENCES

Learning Objectives

Your students should be able to:

- Differentiate between sentence fragments and sentences.
- Unscramble words to make a simple sentence.
- Combine given groups of words to make a simple sentence that makes sense.
- Replace nonsense words in a sentence with words that make sense.
- Write ten simple sentences on given topics.
- Complete each simple sentence with either a single or compound subject.
- Complete each simple sentence with a compound verb.

Directions for Student Study Pages and Practices

Use the student pages (pages 52–71) to help students acquire, reinforce, and review writing simple sentences. They can begin with the activity on page 52 as a review of what they know about simple sentences. Encourage students to check their progress with the Student Progress Assessment Record on page 53. Reproduce the Student Study Pages on pages 54–57 for each student. This section can be used for reference while students do the practices, as well as when they do their own writing.

Pick and choose the practices based on the needs and developmental levels of your students. Answers for the student review practice pages are reproducible, so you may choose to give your students the practice pages, as well as the answer pages, to progress on their own. The answers are on pages 148–152.

Extensions

- Begin by writing sentence scrambles on the board for students. Have students come to the board one at a time and unscramble the sentences. Then ask students to write five scrambled sentences and give their papers to another student. Students can then unscramble each other's sentences.

- You can find refrigerator poetry magnets in many stores. Provide these magnets for your students and invite them to create sentences.

- Write the name of each student on the top of a sheet of paper—one sheet of paper for each student. Then pass the papers around to each student and ask him or her to write one positive statement about the student whose name is at the top of the page. This helps students with sentence writing as well as self-esteem! (Be sure to give each student his or her paper after the activity!)

Name _____

Student Review for Writing Simple Sentences

Directions: For the following sentences, write the number *1* if there is one subject and the number *2* if there are two or more subjects. Underline the subject or subjects.

_____ 1. My brother and his friend like to rollerblade.

_____ 2. Kelsey runs very fast and jumps rope very well.

_____ 3. Karem is a good soccer player.

_____ 4. Lisa, Kristin, Bridget, and Anna came to Melissa's birthday party.

_____ 5. Friends are nice to have.

Directions: For the following sentences, write the number *1* if there is one verb and the number *2* if there are two or more verbs. Then draw a line under the verb or verbs.

_____ 6. The twins ride their bikes to school every day.

_____ 7. Our teacher and principal spoke to us about the writing contest.

_____ 8. The children screamed and cried all day.

_____ 9. The pilot flew the plane above the clouds.

_____ 10. We all laughed and applauded the pilot at the end of our trip.

Directions: Write simple sentences on the back of this paper with the following:

_____ 11. one subject and one verb

_____ 12. two subjects and one verb

_____ 13. one subject and two verbs

_____ 14. two subjects and two verbs

© Good Apple GA13057

Writing Simple Sentences Review

Student Progress Assessment Record

Count how many items you answered correctly in the Student Review for Writing Simple Sentences. Write your score in the *My Score* column. Look at the score in the *Good Score* column. If your score is as high as the good score, you are ready to continue with the next skill. If your score falls below the good score, review the information related to writing simple sentences to make sure you have learned the material. Then move on to the next skill.

Writing Simple Sentences	Good Score	My Score	Review Pages
Subject(s) of Sentences	8–9		
Verb(s) in Sentences	6–7		
Writing Sentences	3–4		

Name_____

Student Study Pages

Writing Simple Sentences

It is important for the sentences you write to make sense. Otherwise your readers will not understand what you are trying to say. Writing simple sentences that are in order and express complete thoughts help give meaning to what you write.

What Are Sentences?

Read the following group of words:

> You do I to want go not.

Does it make sense? Is it a sentence? The answer, of course, is "no" to both questions. **Words in English sentences must be arranged in a certain order for the sentence to make sense.** Read the following group of words:

> I do not want you to go.

Does it make sense? Is it a sentence? The answer is "yes" to both questions. A sentence in English is an orderly arrangement of words that makes sense.

Now read the following groups of words:

> Running around.
> All around the park.
> When she arrives.
> Into the store.
> While I am shopping.
> Rolanda's beautiful little white cat.

Are they sentences? The answer, of course, is "no" because not one of the groups of words expresses a complete thought. **A sentence must express a complete thought.** These are sentence fragments—that is, sentence parts. Read the following groups of words:

> The joggers are jogging all around the park.
> When she arrives, send her to the office immediately.
> Rolanda's beautiful little white cat is lost.

Are the above groups of words sentences? The answer is "yes" because each group of words expresses a complete thought.

Student Study Pages *continued*

Now read the following:
Help!
Don't go.
Stay.
Run!
Remain here with us.
Drive carefully.

Are these sentences? The answer is "yes" because each word or group of words expresses a complete thought. **Notice that a sentence may be as brief as one word if it expresses a complete thought.** In each of these sentences, the subject, *you,* is understood. Each of the sentences has a subject and a verb, and each expresses a complete thought. Each says: *You help! You don't go. You stay. You run! You remain here with us. You drive carefully.*

Special Notes

The **subject** of a sentence is what the sentence is about. The subject can be a person, an animal, a place, a thing, or an idea. In the sentence *Glenn works hard,* "Glenn" is the subject of the sentence. The sentence says something about Glenn.

The **predicate** of a sentence tells something about the subject. The predicate of a sentence is a verb. A **verb** is a telling word—it expresses an action, a state of being, or anything that happens or takes place. A verb can be one word, such as *bake, cook, jump,* or *sew,* or a group of words (verb phrase), such as *am baking, have seen, can sew,* or *will be studying.* In the sentence *Glenn works hard,* the verb *works* tells something about Glenn, the subject of the sentence.

Writing Simple Sentences

Simple Sentences

A **simple sentence** is made up of a word or group of words that names something (subject) and says something about the thing named (predicate). It expresses a complete meaning or thought.

Jack is my best friend.
Caitlin rides her bike to school.
I am happy.

55

Student Study Pages *continued*

A simple sentence consists of one single statement, command, wish, question, or exclamation.

> We are good swimmers.
> Stay where you are.
> Who are you?
> That is great!

Simple Sentences with One Subject and One Verb

A **simple sentence** may consist of a single subject and a single verb. It must express a complete meaning or thought.

> Kelsey plays ball in the park.
> They are not going.
> Andrew likes to swim in the ocean.
> Anthony is writing a play.

Special Notes

A single (one) subject may be either singular or plural. A single subject is singular if it names only one person or thing. For example, *apple, Kelly, Rasheed, he, she,* and *book* are singular. A single subject is plural if it names more than one person or thing. For example, *apples, boys, girls, they,* and *books* are plural. Singular or plural, they are all subjects.

A single subject that names only one person or thing requires a singular verb. For example:

> She *is* going. The circus *is* in town.

A single subject that is plural requires a plural verb. For example:

> They *are* not going. The clowns *are* funny.

Simple Sentences with a Compound Subject and a Single Verb

A simple sentence, which expresses one complete thought, can be written with a compound subject (two or more) and a single verb. The verb in a simple sentence with a compound subject is plural.

> Rebecca and Rachel like to swim.
> Andy, Brian, and Shawn work hard.
> Math, geography, and English are my favorite subjects.
> Recess and lunch are my favorite times.

Student Study Pages *continued*

Simple Sentences with a Single Subject and a Compound Verb

A simple sentence, which expresses one complete thought, can be written with a single subject and a compound verb.

> The children run and play.
> Marie plays the piano and sings very well.
> Jim jogs and plays basketball every day.
> Camille works hard, plays hard, and eats a lot.
> They ate too much and got sick.

Simple Sentences with a Compound Subject and a Compound Verb

A simple sentence can be written with a compound subject and a compound verb. The verb in a simple sentence with a compound subject is plural.

> Huma and Noma are rushing to the auditorium and are trying out for the play.
> The teachers and students have met and discussed their differences.
> The snow, rain, and sleet blanket the roads and make them slippery.

Name_____

Practice 1

Directions: Read each of the following carefully and decide whether it is a sentence or a sentence fragment. Underline each complete sentence. Rewrite any sentence fragment so that it is a complete sentence.

Remember: A sentence must express a complete thought. It should also contain a subject and a verb.

1. Play._____

_____

2. Don't go there. _____

_____

3. He reads._____

_____

4. A funny movie. _____

_____

5. Rachel plays tennis very well._____

_____

6. The game is set for tomorrow._____

_____

7. Who are they?_____

_____

8. I can't go._____

_____

9. When they arrive._____

_____

10. And in the woods._____

_____

Name_____

Practice 2

Directions: Read the following paragraph carefully. Notice that some parts of the paragraph are not meaningful sentences. Underline each sentence fragment. Then write a simple sentence for each sentence fragment. You may combine sentence parts to make a simple sentence, and you may change word forms, add words, or leave out words as long as the idea does not change.

Many years ago, the great magician Merlin, looking. Like a beggar. Stopped at a peasant's cottage one evening. He was given a hearty welcome. The wife brought out. Some fresh bread and milk for him. This pleased Merlin. Being a magician. Merlin decided. To reward them.

_____

_____

_____

_____

_____

_____

_____

_____

Name _____

Practice 3

Directions: Here are ten scrambled sentences. Unscramble and rewrite each sentence so it makes sense.

1. To I bike ride school a.

_____

2. Me help.

_____

3. Do where you live?

_____

4. Friends my friendly are and to with be fun.

_____

5. Do tricks zoo in the animals the.

_____

6. Head clown circus the on in the stood his.

_____

7. Driver race intend be in I to the the.

_____

8. Olympics intend be in I to the.

_____

9. One knew do to no what.

_____

10. Two allowance my gone is always in days.

_____

reproducible *60* © Good Apple GA13057

Name _____

Practice 4

Directions: Here are eight scrambled sentences. Unscramble and rewrite each sentence so it makes sense.

1. Are going you where?

_____

2. Subject reading my best is.

_____

3. Team the won game our basketball.

_____

4. Party having are house we a my at.

_____

5. Leaving beach we tomorrow are for the.

_____

6. Lot headache I homework have bad a a of and.

_____

7. Days my in friend is best two having birthday a party.

_____

8. Tour in summer we the going are United to States the.

_____

Name_____

Practice 5

Directions: Choose one word or group of words from Column 1 and a group of words from Column 2 to make a simple sentence that makes sense. Each group of words from Column 2 may be used once. Write the sentences below.

Column 1

_____ 1. Craig

_____ 2. They

_____ 3. No one

_____ 4. The other students

_____ 5. I

_____ 6. The teacher

_____ 7. Everyone

_____ 8. Which person

_____ 9. He

_____ 10. Life

Column 2

a. are not very friendly to him.

b. feel sorry for him.

c. must be difficult for him.

d. is a new student in our class.

e. needs help.

f. ignore him.

g. ever chooses him for anything.

h. has tried to help him in class.

i. will help him?

j. makes fun of him.

1. _____

2. _____

3. _____

4. _____

5. _____

6. _____

7. _____

8. _____

9. _____

10. _____

Name_____

Practice 6

Directions: Here are five nonsense sentences. Read each sentence carefully. Cross out the nonsense words and use your own words to rewrite each sentence so it makes sense.

1. After the cloomp, Helm will go to the sert.

_____

_____

2. Stop pluf!

_____

_____

3. Jisk is a jolly vern.

_____

_____

4. The fleek turned a neto.

_____

_____

5. Vanessa bleeped for jers.

_____

_____

Name_____

Practice 7

Directions: Write ten simple sentences that make sense. The phrases in parentheses tell you what to write the sentences about. Use the back of the paper if you need more room to write.

1. (a favorite animal)

_____

2. (a favorite sport)

_____

3. (a favorite book)

_____

4. (something you dislike)

_____

5. (something funny)

_____

6. (a rainy day)

_____

7. (a mean person)

_____

8. (a favorite television show)

_____

9. (a wish)

_____

10. (a career choice)

_____

Name _____

Practice 8

Directions: Here are ten incomplete simple sentences. Insert a single or compound subject in the blank for each incomplete sentence to create a sentence that makes sense.

1. _____ are not going to the picnic with us.

2. _____ has a bad cold.

3. _____ are enjoyable sports.

4. My _____ cries too much.

5. Whose _____ do you have?

6. Anna's _____ does not include that.

7. _____ is a good sport.

8. _____ play soccer very well.

9. Are _____ going to the party?

10. _____ needs to have more confidence in herself.

Name_____

Practice 9

Directions: Here are five nonsense sentences. Read each sentence carefully. Cross out the nonsense words and use your own words to rewrite each sentence so it makes sense.

1. The bright red bloob and the deep bleep needed care immediately.

_____

_____

2. Susan and Tony feible a lot.

_____

_____

3. Richard deebles baseball every day.

_____

_____

4. Treibe and Trob like to do that.

_____

_____

5. Bandle, Moisle, and Weigle argue too much.

_____

_____

Name_____

Practice 10

Directions: Choose a group of words from Column 1 and a group of words from Column 2 to make a simple sentence that makes sense. Each group of words from Column 2 may be used once. Write the sentences below.

Column 1

_____ 1. Slappy, the clown, and Slerpy, the dog,

_____ 2. The mixed-up cat and the helpful mouse

_____ 3. The ferocious lion and its trainer

_____ 4. The dinosaur and the flying serpent

_____ 5. Superman and Batman

_____ 6. Sun and water

_____ 7. The bus and train

_____ 8. Fruits and vegetables

_____ 9. The mongoose and the cobra

_____ 10. Raisins and prunes

Column 2

a. are comic book characters.

b. are needed for plants.

c. are the foods of vegetarians.

d. perform together.

e. are natural enemies.

f. play together.

g. thrill the audience.

h. no longer exist.

i. are dried fruits.

j. are common means of public transportation.

1. _____

2. _____

3. _____

4. _____

5. _____

6. _____

7. _____

8. _____

9. _____

10. _____

Name _____

Practice 11

Directions: Choose a word or a group of words from Column 1 and a group of words from Column 2 to make a simple sentence that makes sense. Each group of words from Column 2 may be used once. Write the sentences below.

Column 1

_____ 1. The good fairy

_____ 2. Clever Gretel

_____ 3. The golden bird

_____ 4. Rapunzel

_____ 5. The old woman in the woods

_____ 6. The little match girl

_____ 7. The six swans

_____ 8. The three spinners

_____ 9. The six travelers

_____ 10. Jack the Giant Killer

Column 2

a. dropped from the sky and flew about the queen.

b. ran after the girl and caught her.

c. entered and refreshed themselves.

d. laughed and laid a golden egg.

e. seized the trumpet and blew a great blast.

f. smiled and touched the child with her wand.

g. tricked the witch.

h. started to sing and let down her hair.

i. entered, sat down, and began to spin.

j. waited for someone to buy her wares.

1. _____

2. _____

3. _____

4. _____

5. _____

6. _____

7. _____

8. _____

9. _____

10. _____

Name _____

Practice 12

Directions: Complete each sentence below with a compound verb to make a simple sentence that makes sense.

1. We _____

_____

2. Machines _____

_____

3. The peculiar bird _____

_____

4. Some people _____

_____

5. The cross-eyed animal _____

_____

6. A bowlegged duck _____

_____

7. The clown _____

_____

8. The accused man _____

_____

9. The winner of the contest _____

_____

10. The athlete _____

_____

Name _____

Practice 13

Directions: Choose a group of words from Column 1 and a group of words from Column 2 to make a simple sentence that makes sense. Each group of words from Column 2 may be used once. Write the sentences below.

Column 1

_____ 1. A little girl and her godmother

_____ 2. The golden bird and the golden horse

_____ 3. The wicked brother and the fox

_____ 4. The king and queen

_____ 5. A sea captain and his friends

_____ 6. The dancing dog and the meowing cat

_____ 7. The princess and her sister

_____ 8. The princess and the miller boy

_____ 9. Tom Thumb and the mouse

_____ 10. A giant and a dwarf

Column 2

a. were found and imprisoned.

b. run and play all day.

c. played and had fun.

d. plucked and ate the forbidden apple.

e. spin and weave for a living.

f. met and fought.

g. greeted and kissed the princess.

h. got into the coach and rode away.

i. laughed and joked.

j. did not fly and did not run.

1. _____

2. _____

3. _____

4. _____

5. _____

6. _____

7. _____

8. _____

9. _____

10. _____

Name_____

Practice 14

Directions: Fill in each blank to make a simple sentence with a compound verb. The sentence may be a nonsense or silly sentence.

1. Snoopy, the bear, and Snooky, the clown, _____

_____ .

2. Charlotte, the spider, and Wilbur, the pig, _____

_____ .

3. The camel without a hump and the elephant without a trunk _____

_____ .

4. Jack and his magic carpet _____

_____ .

5. Dorothy and the witch _____

_____ .

6. Loretta and Irina _____

_____ .

7. The scarecrow and the robot _____

_____ .

8. The aliens and earthlings _____

_____ .

9. Anthony, Juliet, and Scrubby, the silent dog, _____

_____ .

10. A wizard and a witch _____

_____ .

COMPOUND SENTENCES

Explanation

A **compound sentence** contains two or more independent clauses (groups of words that can stand alone as complete sentences) but no dependent clauses (groups of words that cannot stand alone as sentences). For example:

> The rain fell, and the wind blew.
> The music majors attended the concert, and the theater majors went to the dance.

Each of the above sentences contains two independent clauses. Each independent clause can stand alone as a simple sentence because each clause has a subject and a predicate, and each expresses a complete thought.

> The rain fell.
> The wind blew.
> The music majors attended the concert.
> The theater majors went to the dance.

In a compound sentence, each independent clause has its own subject, and each subject has its own independent verb. As a result, each compound sentence is made up of independent clauses that express different ideas.

Two independent clauses may be joined by certain linking words called **coordinate (equal) conjunctions** (words that connect phrases, clauses, and other words) to form compound sentences. The most often used coordinate conjunctions are the words *and, but,* and *or.* The words *nor, for,* and *yet* are also used as coordinate conjunctions.

> Take care of yourself now, or you will suffer the consequences later.
> I wanted to go away to school, but my family needed me at home.

Coordinate conjunctions connect groups of words that have the same importance. The linking word *and* is used to add one idea to another. The words *but* and *yet* are used for contrast, the word *or* is used to separate ideas that are choices or alternatives, the word *nor* is used to separate ideas that are negative choices, and the word *for* is used to show the cause or proof of a statement. When the words *and, but, or, for, yet,* and *nor* are used to join two independent clauses, a comma is usually used before the linking word.

Sometimes linking words are pairs of words called **correlative conjunctions—** linking words that show a one-to-one relation between two sets of things. The words *either . . . or* and *neither . . . nor* are two pairs of correlative conjunctions that are commonly used to connect independent clauses.

> Either we do what they say, or we will be hurt.

Other linking words that can be used to connect independent clauses are *also, accordingly, besides, however, moreover, nevertheless, so, still, then, therefore, thus, consequently,* and so on. For example:

> We waited for them for two hours; then they finally arrived.
> These people helped us capture the criminals; therefore, we should
> reward them.

When linking words, such as *therefore, so, nevertheless, however, moreover,* and so on, are used to join two independent clauses, a semicolon usually is used before the linking word. However, for the linking word *so,* either a comma or a semicolon may be used.

Special Note

Conjunctive adverbs are used both as modifiers and linking words. They function as both adverbs and conjunctions. Some examples of conjunctive adverbs are the words *accordingly, consequently, however, therefore, furthermore, so, then, nevertheless, besides,* and *moreover.* Conjunctive adverbs are used to connect two independent clauses and thus form compound sentences. The conjunctive adverb that connects two independent clauses modifies the second clause as a whole and connects it with the preceding one.

> We went to so much trouble to obtain this position for your brother;
> nevertheless, he is not happy.

During or by the end of the intermediate grades, students are able to:

- master all items of previous years.
- write compound sentences.
- recognize that a compound sentence contains two or more groups of words that can stand alone as sentences. Each group must have its own subject and verb.
- recognize that each compound sentence has two groups of words that can stand alone as a simple sentence because each has a subject and a verb, and each expresses a complete thought.

- use a comma with a conjunction such as *and* or *but* to combine two sentences into a compound sentence.
- avoid the overuse of conjunctions in writing sentences.
- avoid certain unacceptable sentence fragments such as *Into the store* and *When she came.*
- recognize that the careful placement of words is important to gain clarity in sentence writing.
- write compound sentences using linking words such as *however, therefore,* and *nevertheless* with a semicolon before the linking word.

Modeling Strategy

Here is how one teacher models for her students how to write compound sentences. The teacher tells the students that she has noticed many of them joining two sentences together with just a comma. She tells them that when they combine two simple sentences together with just a comma, they are writing run-on sentences. She will teach them how to write compound sentences correctly. She then tells them that a compound sentence is the joining of two simple sentences. The teacher writes the following sentences on the chalkboard.

I have a lot of homework.
It's too late to do it now.

She says, "I will model for you how I put these two simple sentences together to make a compound sentence. Each sentence can stand alone because each expresses a complete thought, and each has a subject and a predicate.

"If I join the two together with a comma, I must use a linking word such as *and, or, but, for,* or *so* with the comma. Let me show you what I mean. Here are two sentences. I want to make them into a compound sentence. I can do this by joining my two sentences with the linking word *but* and putting a comma before *but.* For example:

I have a lot of homework, but it's too late to do it now.

"I like the compound sentence better than having two separate simple sentences."

The teacher then tells her students that there are other ways to combine two simple sentences to make a compound sentence. She says, "I could also use a linking word, such as *however, moreover, nevertheless,* or *therefore,* to link two sentences together. If I use these linking words, I must use a semicolon before the linking word and a comma after it. Let me give you an example using the same sentences as before:

> I have a lot of homework.
> It's too late to do it now.

"In looking at my sentences, I see that the linking word that will express the meaning I want is *however.*

> I have a lot of homework; however, it's too late to do it now.

"Does anyone have any questions about what I have done to link two simple sentences together?" the teacher asks. She then gives her students several sentences and a list of linking words, and has them combine the simple sentences using the linking words.

Learning Objectives

Your students should be able to:

- Differentiate between compound and simple sentences.
- Choose words to make a compound sentence.
- Combine two sentences into one compound sentence, using a coordinate conjunction.
- Construct five compound sentences, using a coordinate conjunction.
- Combine two sentences into one using a linking word such as *however, therefore,* or *nevertheless.*
- Construct five compound sentences using a linking word such as *therefore, however,* or *nevertheless.*

Directions for Student Study Pages and Practices

Use the student pages (pages 77–87) to help students acquire, reinforce, and review writing compound sentences. Reproduce the Student Study Pages on pages 77 and 78 for each student. This section can be used for reference while students do the practices, as well as when they do their own writing.

Pick and choose the practices based on the needs and developmental levels of your students. Answers for the practice pages are reproducible, so you may choose to give your students the practice pages, as well as the answer pages, to progress on their own. The answers are on pages 152–154.

Extensions

■ Write several simple sentences on heavy paper or poster board. Cut out each sentence. Invite students to use the sentences to make as many compound sentences as they can. You may want to divide the group into teams and have each team create as many sentences as they can in a specific amount of time.

■ Give each student a page from the newspaper and ask them to cut out as many compound sentences as they can find in the text. Students can then use the sentences to make up interesting news items of their own.

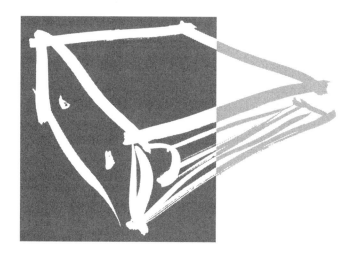

Student Study Pages

Compound Sentences

Writing a Compound Sentence

A **compound sentence** is made up of two or more simple sentences. For example:

> My brother is a senior in high school, and my sister is a sophomore
> in college.
> My best friend is a lot of fun, but he is not very reliable.

Writing Compound Sentences Using Coordinate Conjunctions

Two simple sentences may be joined by linking words called **conjunctions** to form compound sentences. Conjunctions that connect groups of words that have the same importance are called **coordinate (equal) conjunctions.**

The most often used coordinate conjunctions are the words *and, but,* and *or.* The words *nor, for,* and *yet* are also used as conjunctions. When conjunctions such as *and, but, for,* or *or* are used to connect two simple sentences to form a compound sentence, a comma is usually used before the conjunction. For example:

> Sharon is a good piano player, *and* her sister is a good violin player.
> Alfredo wanted to go to the movies, *but* his friend did not.
> Chris must work harder in school, *or* he will fail two subjects.
> Tawanda is well liked, *for* she is always cheerful.

The coordinate conjunctions *and, but,* and *or* are most commonly used to connect words as well as groups of words. For example:

> 1. I like to ski.　　　　2. I like to dance.
> 1. Jane is pretty.　　　　2. Mary is pretty.
> 1. Jim can go.　　　　　2. George can go.

These sentences can be combined to form simple sentences using the coordinate conjunctions *and* or *or.*

> I like to ski *and* dance.
> Jane *and* Mary are pretty.
> Jim *or* George can go.

Student Study Pages *continued*

The pairs of simple sentences presented as examples can be combined to form compound sentences.

> I like to ski, and I like to dance.
> Jane is pretty, and Mary is pretty.
> Jim can go, or George can go.

However, for these examples, the shortened, combined simple sentences are preferable to the longer combined compound sentences.

In the following examples, the pairs of sentences cannot be shortened, but they can be combined to form compound sentences.

> 1. I like to play the piano.   2. No one will listen to me.
>
>   I like to play the piano, but no one will listen to me.
>
> 1. We opened the window.   2. A bird flew in.
>
>   We opened the window, and a bird flew in.
>
> 1. Dress more quickly.   2. We will be late.
>
>   Dress more quickly, or we will be late.

Writing Compound Sentences Using Linking Words

A compound sentence is made up of two or more simple sentences. Linking words such as *also, accordingly, besides, therefore, however, nevertheless, then, moreover, so,* and so on can be used to connect simple sentences to form a compound sentence. For example:

> John made the most points in the game; therefore, he should receive the award.
> Everything started out very well; however, it turned out disastrously.

Special Note

When linking words such as *therefore, nevertheless, then, moreover,* and *however* are used to join two simple sentences, a semicolon (;) usually is used before the linking word. For the linking word *so,* a comma or a semicolon may be used before the linking word. However, a comma is more often used with the word *so.*

Name _____

Practice 1

Directions: Write a *C* in front of the compound sentences and an *S* in front of the simple sentences.

_____ 1. Jim and Carol went skiing and sledding.

_____ 2. The twins are hard workers and good businessmen.

_____ 3. Jenny and Doug went for a long walk in the woods.

_____ 4. Carlos jogs every evening, and his wife jogs every morning.

_____ 5. Every one of us was exhausted and famished.

_____ 6. No one said anything, yet we knew how they felt.

_____ 7. We opened the window, and then a bird flew in.

_____ 8. The sun came out, but it was still raining.

_____ 9. The rain made the wilted flowers spring back to life.

_____ 10. We had forgotten our promise to ourselves about turning over a new leaf.

Name_____

Practice 2

Directions: Choose the group of words that makes the sentence a compound sentence. Write the sentence in the space below.

Example: We fished all day
          (a) but caught nothing;
          (b) and had a lot of fun;
          (c) and we had a good time.

Answer: (c) We fished all day, and we had a good time.

1. My brother is (a) very popular and a good student; (b) popular and smart; (c) not too popular, but I like him.

_____

_____

2. Many persons saw (a) the attacker mug the victim; (b) the attacker, but they refused to identify him; (c) the attacker but did nothing about him.

_____

_____

3. The people were (a) afraid of the attacker; (b) ashamed of themselves for their cowardice; (c) ashamed of themselves, but they were too frightened.

_____

_____

4. One of my friends saw (a) the attack, but his mother would not let him testify; (b) the attack and tried to help the victim; (c) the whole thing and called the police.

_____

_____

5. Today is (a) the day of the picnic and the big game; (b) the day of the picnic and the big game, but it's raining; (c) the day of the picnic and the big game at our school.

_____

_____

Name _____

Practice 3

Directions: Choose the group of words that makes the sentence a compound sentence. Write the sentence in the space below.

1. I enjoy math, (a) but I don't do well in it at school; (b) and do very well in it at school; (c) but don't do very well in it at school.

   _____

   _____

2. My father is (a) an FBI agent and an expert in decoding cryptic messages; (b) an FBI agent, and he is an expert decoder of cryptic messages; (c) an FBI agent but doesn't carry a gun.

   _____

   _____

3. I enjoy watching television, (a) especially the comedy shows; (b) but not the commercials; (c) but the commercials bother me.

   _____

   _____

4. The show was (a) very gruesome and frightening; (b) not very educational or helpful; (c) funny, but we didn't like it.

   _____

   _____

5. Vacations are (a) my favorite times but very tiring; (b) my favorite times, and I make the most of them; (c) fun and filled with lots of adventure.

   _____

   _____

Name _____

Practice 4

Directions: Here are pairs of sentences. Choose a coordinate conjunction, such as *and, but, or, yet,* or *for,* and combine the two sentences into one compound sentence. Write the sentence in the space below. For example:

My brother wants to be on the basketball team.
He is too short.
My brother wants to be on the basketball team, but he is too short.

1. My sister Jane is an excellent student.
   My sister Mary does not do well in school.

   _____

   _____

2. Only three of my friends went to the party.
   They were the only ones invited.

   _____

   _____

3. My brother is dating my best girlfriend.
   My sister is dating my best friend's brother.

   _____

   _____

4. It became cloudy.
   It started to rain.

   _____

   _____

5. She deserves the punishment.
   I feel sorry for her.

   _____

   _____

Name_____

Practice 5

Directions: Here are pairs of sentences. Choose a coordinate conjunction, such as *and, but, or, yet,* or *for,* and combine the two sentences into one compound sentence. Write the sentence in the space below.

1. The test was hard.
    I did very well on it.

    _____

    _____

2. The tall trees looked like soldiers standing at attention.
    The flowers looked like pretty maidens dancing in the breeze.

    _____

    _____

3. John was outmatched in the set.
    He won.

    _____

    _____

4. Sharon is going to the shore during school break.
    She is going to the mountains.

    _____

    _____

5. Jennifer is a cheerful and happy person.
    Everyone likes her.

    _____

    _____

Name_____

Practice 6

Directions: Write five compound sentences using a coordinate conjunction such as *and, but, or, nor, for,* or *yet.* Make sure your compound sentence is made up of two or more simple sentences.

1. _____

_____

_____

2. _____

_____

_____

3. _____

_____

_____

4. _____

_____

_____

5. _____

_____

_____

Name_____

Practice 7

Directions: Here are pairs of sentences. Choose a linking word, such as *however, then, therefore, nevertheless, also,* or *besides,* and combine the two sentences into one compound sentence. Don't forget to put a semicolon before the linking word. Write the sentence in the space below. For example:

> It rained on the day of the school picnic.
> We postponed it.
> It rained on the day of the school picnic; therefore, we postponed it.

1. I don't like the plan.
   I will not go along with you.

   _____

   _____

2. That doesn't sound too exciting.
   I may still go.

   _____

   _____

3. The class entered the auditorium and sat down.
   The new instructor came in.

   _____

   _____

4. My parents don't like some of my friends.
   I invite them to my house.

   _____

   _____

5. Last year I received all As.
   This year I'm failing two subjects.

   _____

   _____

Name_____

Practice 8

Directions: Here are pairs of sentences. Choose a linking word, such as *however, then, therefore, nevertheless, also,* or *besides,* and combine the two sentences into one compound sentence. Write the sentence in the space below.

1. We watered the plants.
   We fertilized them.

   _____

   _____

2. All of my friends are champion ice skaters.
   Not one of them wanted to enter the contest.

   _____

   _____

3. I prefer to stay out of politics.
   I was nominated to run for class president.

   _____

   _____

4. My campaign manager is excellent.
   I have a good chance of winning.

   _____

   _____

5. At the beginning, everyone promises to run a clean campaign.
   By the end, it usually becomes pretty muddy.

   _____

   _____

Name_____

Practice 9

Directions: Write five compound sentences using a linking word such as *however, then, therefore, nevertheless,* or *besides.*

1. _____

_____

_____

2. _____

_____

_____

3. _____

_____

_____

4. _____

_____

_____

5. _____

_____

_____

ADVANCED SENTENCE WRITING SKILLS

The sentence writing skills presented in Sections 5 and 6 are usually introduced in grades six to eight. When teachers introduce these sentence writing skills will depend, however, on the individual differences of their students.

Section
5

COMPLEX SENTENCES

Explanation

A **complex sentence** contains one independent clause and one or more dependent clauses. An example of a complex sentence follows:

> Although John is a good athlete, he does not spend too much time in sports.

The independent clause in the above sentence is *he does not spend too much time in sports.* The dependent clause is *Although John is a good athlete.* Here is another example of a complex sentence:

> Since that happened a long time ago, when she was very young, I wouldn't hold it against her.

The independent clause of the above sentence is *I wouldn't hold it against her.* The dependent clauses are *Since that happened a long time ago, when she was very young.*

Linking words called **subordinate (dependent) conjunctions** connect dependent clauses with their independent clauses to form complex sentences. The most often used subordinate conjunctions are the words *although, as, because, before, if, since, that, unless, until, after, as if, as though, as soon as, in order that, even if,* and *so that.*

> Although he said that he was not angry, he left immediately.
> Alisa will not walk again unless the operation is a success.

Subordinate conjunctions are used to show more involved relations than coordinate conjunctions, such as *and, but, or,* and *for,* which are used to form compound sentences.

Other words such as *where, when,* and *while* often function as subordinate conjunctions.

> They didn't say where they were going.
> When you see Joe, tell him I can't attend the meeting.
> While I am in charge, no one will be treated badly.

Pronouns such as *who, which, that,* and *what* also function as subordinate conjunctions to relate a dependent or subordinate clause to its main or principal clause.

I don't understand the problem that we did in class.
The students who are in my history class are all experts.

Special Notes

Dependent clauses introduced by a subordinate conjunction cannot stand alone as sentences, though they contain a subject and a verb. They are only sentence fragments, because they do not express complete thoughts. For example: *When he arrived; Although I may go; Before I speak; Because the dance was fun; Since the hour is near.*

The words *when* and *where* are not always subordinate conjunctions used to introduce a dependent clause. These words can begin a question sentence when they are at the beginning of the sentence. For example: *When are you going? Where are you going?*

A comma is usually used after a dependent clause when it comes before an independent clause in a complex sentence. For example: *When they arrived, we were prepared for them. Although she is good in sports, she does not like to practice too much.*

A comma is used when a dependent clause follows an independent clause if the dependent clause is **nonrestrictive** (provides additional rather than essential information). For example:

She likes parties, while I prefer solitary walking.

While I prefer . . . cannot stand alone and is therefore a dependent clause. But it does not add information that limits the statement *She likes parties.*

Clauses introduced by the words *though* or *although* are always nonrestrictive.

You ought to visit Stone Mountain, although it is a little out of your way.

A comma is not used between an independent clause and a following dependent clause if the dependent clause is **restrictive** (provides essential information). For example:

He should not go on hay rides if he's allergic to hay.

Clauses introduced by the word *if* are always restrictive. *If he's allergic to hay* restricts to a single reason why he should not go on hay rides.

In the sentence *Set the table while the meat is broiling,* the word *while* restricts the time of the main verb—*set.*

More Examples:

Sally will not come unless the sun shines.

Unless . . . is a condition restricting the main clause.

Loosen the nuts so that the wheel turns freely.

So that . . . is a clause restricting the main clause to a specific purpose.

The wheel will spin freely on its axle, so that any misalignment will show clearly as a pronounced wobble.

The words *so that* introduce a dependent clause that describes a result of what is stated in the main clause. The result, however, imposes no restriction on the main clause—*the wheel will spin freely, no matter what happens.* The clause is therefore nonrestrictive and takes a comma.

Learning Objectives

Your students should be able to:

- Differentiate between simple, compound, and complex sentences.
- Choose words to make a complex sentence.
- Combine two sentences into one complex sentence.
- Construct five complex sentences.
- Construct five complex sentences in which the dependent clause precedes the independent clause.
- Construct five complex sentences in which the independent clause precedes the dependent clause.

Directions for Student Study Pages and Practices

Use the student pages (pages 93–102) to help students acquire, reinforce, and review writing complex sentences. Reproduce the Student Study Pages on pages 93 and 94 for each student. This section can be used for reference while students do the practices, as well as when they do their own writing.

Pick and choose the practices based on the needs and developmental levels of your students. Answers for the practice pages are reproducible, so you may choose to give your students the practice pages, as well as the answer pages, to progress on their own. The answers are on pages 154 and 55.

COMPLEX SENTENCES

Extensions

■ Write out the the following linking words and phrases on slips of paper: *although, as, because, before, if, since, that, unless, until, after, as if, as though, as soon as, in order that, even if, so that, where, when, while, who, which, that,* and *what.* Then ask students to write out several sentences and cut them out. Each student then chooses a linking word from a hat or box and uses that word to link one of the sentences with a sentence written by another student.

■ Divide the group into teams. One member from one team writes a simple sentence on the board. Then a member from the other team must use a linking word and another simple sentence or clause to make it into a complex sentence. Encourage teams to try to stump each other with their sentences.

92

© Good Apple GA13057

Student Study Pages

Complex Sentences

A **complex sentence** is made up of one simple sentence and one or more groups of words that cannot stand alone as sentences. In order to understand a complex sentence, you must be familiar with the terms *independent clause* and *dependent clause*. A **clause** is a group of words that contains both a subject and a predicate.

Independent clause

A clause that makes an independent statement is called an **independent clause.** An independent clause can stand alone as a simple sentence because it expresses a complete thought. For example, *Kelsey is pretty,* and *Peter is handsome. (Kelsey is pretty* is an independent clause, and *Peter is handsome* is also an independent clause.)

Dependent clause

A clause that is not by itself complete in meaning is called a **dependent clause.** A dependent clause cannot stand alone as a sentence because it does not express a complete thought. For example, *Although he is very tall, he didn't make the basketball team. (Although he is very tall* is a dependent clause, and *he didn't make the basketball team* is an independent clause.)

A complex sentence contains one independent clause (a group of words that can stand alone as a sentence) and one or more dependent clauses (a group of words that cannot stand alone as a sentence).

> When the student leader appeared onstage, everyone started to applaud.
> Although I do not agree with all of her views, I will vote for her.
> Since that took place a long time ago, I will not hold it against you.

Each of the above sentences has one independent clause and one dependent clause. In the first example, the independent clause is *everyone started to applaud;* the dependent clause is *When the student leader appeared onstage.* In the second example, the independent clause is *I will vote for her;* the dependent clause is *Although I do not agree with all of her views.* In the third example, the independent clause is *I will not hold it against you;* the dependent clause is *Since that took place a long time ago.*

Student Study Pages *continued*

Subordinate Conjunction

Linking words, called **subordinate (dependent) conjunctions,** connect dependent clauses with their independent clauses to form complex sentences. The most often used subordinate conjunctions are: *although, as, because, before, if, since, that, unless, until, after, as if, as though, even though, even if, as soon as,* and *so that.* Other words, such as *where, when,* and *while,* often function as subordinate conjunctions as well.

> When you come back from the store, we will go to the movies.
> While we were at Rachel's house, we did our homework.

Pronouns such as *who, which, that,* and *what* can also function as subordinate conjunctions to connect a dependent clause to an independent clause.

> She didn't know which one she liked.
> I didn't understand the homework assignment that our teacher gave us.

Special Notes

Note that each independent clause in a complex sentence can stand alone as a separate sentence, and that each dependent clause cannot stand alone as a separate sentence. A dependent clause is called *dependent* because it depends on the independent clause to complete its meaning.

Dependent clauses are also called **subordinate clauses,** and independent clauses are also called **main** or **principal clauses**. A comma is usually used after a dependent clause when it comes before an independent clause in a complex sentence. For example:

> When Al entered the class twenty minutes late, everyone turned to
>   look at him.
> After I studied hard for the exam, I was exhausted.

Name_____

Practice 1

Directions: Write an *S* in front of the simple sentences, a *C* in front of the compound sentences, and an *X* in front of the complex sentences. Underline the dependent clause in each complex sentence.

_____ 1. After we went for a long walk in the park, we were famished.

_____ 2. Everyone was exhausted, but no one would admit it

_____ 3. My brother and sister are always fighting about something.

_____ 4. I hate it that I am the youngest in my class.

_____ 5. My best friend loves to rollerblade.

_____ 6. Every one of my friends is looking forward to the summer.

_____ 7. No one knows what he or she will be doing in the summer.

_____ 8. My sister wants to be a doctor when she grows up.

_____ 9. I would also like to be a doctor, but I can't stand the sight of blood.

_____ 10. Although she practices a lot, she doesn't play the piano very well.

Name_____

Practice 2

Directions: Choose the group of words that makes each sentence complex. Write the sentence in the space below.

1. We had (a) fun at the party and didn't want to go home; (b) a good time at the party; however, we were exhausted; (c) fun at the party, even though we hadn't wanted to go.

_____

_____

2. We were (a) frightened when we came home and found the windows and doors open; (b) frightened and didn't know what to do; (c) frightened; therefore, we called the police.

_____

_____

3. No one knew (a) about the robberies for a long time; (b) about the robberies because the victims were away on vacation; (c) about the robberies; therefore, no one called the police.

_____

_____

4. Seth is (a) an excellent tennis player, and Andrew is an excellent golfer; (b) interested in sports but not in fishing or hunting; (c) interested in sports, even if his best friend isn't.

_____

_____

5. The entertainment during the intermission was (a) better than the main event; (b) not very good, until the comedians came on; (c) not as good as last year's, but it was amusing.

_____

_____

Name_____

Practice 3

Directions: Choose the group of words that makes each sentence complex. Write the sentence in the space below.

1. The players were (a) exhausted, but they wouldn't give up; (b) disappointed that they lost the game; (c) unsure of themselves on the field, and they made lots of errors.

   _____

   _____

2. It is (a) funny and sad at the same time; (b) not funny to me, but it is to the others; (c) amusing because it makes him look like a fool.

   _____

   _____

3. Lots of people try (a) different remedies but to no avail; (b) hard, even though there is no chance for success; (c) different things, but they usually do not succeed.

   _____

   _____

4. The animals in the zoo were (a) in a good mood, for they had just eaten; (b) not happy that the people were not feeding them; (c) acting silly and making lots of noise.

   _____

   _____

5. The students had (a) mixed feelings about the teacher when he gave them the surprise exam; (b) no problems with the exam; (c) anger for the teacher but said nothing.

   _____

   _____

97

Name _____

Practice 4

Directions: Here are pairs of sentences. Choose a subordinate conjunction from the list that follows, and combine each pair of sentences into one complex sentence. Write the sentence in the space below.

after, although, as, because, before, if, since, that, unless, until, when, while, as if, as soon as, as though, even if, even though, in order that

Example: We arrived late at school. We could not find our class.

When we arrived late at school, we could not find our class.

1. The children were playing in the yard.
   They saw a huge bird.

_____

_____

2. My brother is a hard worker.
   He does not seem to be able to get ahead.

_____

_____

3. I will be elected class president.
   I will not change my views about that topic.

_____

_____

4. He is well liked.
   He is always helpful, kind, and considerate.

_____

_____

5. The protesters were allowed to picket.
   No one agreed with their views.

_____

_____

Name_____

Practice 5

Directions: Here are pairs of sentences. Choose a subordinate conjunction from the list that follows, and combine each pair of sentences into one complex sentence. Write the sentence in the space below.

after, although, as, because, before, if, since, that, unless, until, when, while, as if, as soon as, as though, even if, even though, in order that

1. I could definitely use the money.
   I will not earn it that way.

   _____

   _____

2. My friends are a lot of fun to be with.
   They kid me a lot.

   _____

   _____

3. Help is on the way.
   We should try to do something now.

   _____

   _____

4. I will work very hard.
   You have so much faith in me.

   _____

   _____

5. We all got off the train.
   A crowd of people rushed toward us.

   _____

   _____

Name_____

Practice 6

Directions: Write five complex sentences using a subordinate conjunction.

1. _____

_____

_____

2. _____

_____

_____

3. _____

_____

_____

4. _____

_____

_____

5. _____

_____

_____

Name _____

Practice 7

Directions: Write five complex sentences in which the dependent clause comes before the independent clause.

    Example: When the police arrived, the crowd left.

1. _____

_____

_____

2. _____

_____

_____

3. _____

_____

_____

4. _____

_____

_____

5. _____

_____

_____

Name_____

Practice 8

Directions: Write five complex sentences in which the independent clause comes before the dependent clause.

>   **Example:** Everyone was excited when the famous actor came to visit
>   our class.

1. _____

_____

_____

2. _____

_____

_____

3. _____

_____

_____

4. _____

_____

_____

5. _____

_____

_____

COMPOUND-COMPLEX SENTENCES

Explanation

A **compound-complex sentence** is made up of two or more independent clauses and one or more dependent clauses. For example:

> When the train stopped abruptly, some people fell on other people, and some people landed on the floor.

The independent clauses in this sentence are *some people fell on other people* and *some people landed on the floor*. The dependent clause is *When the train stopped abruptly*.

> The announcement was made and, as the president entered, there was a great cheer.

The independent clauses in the above sentence are *The announcement was made* and *there was a great cheer*. The dependent clause is *as the president entered*.

Learning Objectives

Your students should be able to:

- Differentiate between simple, compound, complex, and compound-complex sentences.
- Choose words to make a compound-complex sentence.
- Combine a group of sentences into one compound-complex sentence.
- Construct five compound-complex sentences.

Directions for Student Study Page and Practices

Use the student pages (pages 105–111) to help students acquire, reinforce, and review writing compound-complex sentences. Reproduce the Student Study Page on page 105 for each student. This section can be used for reference while students do the practices, as well as when they do their own writing.

Pick and choose the practices based on the needs and developmental levels of your students. Answers for the practice pages are reproducible, so you may choose to give your students the practice pages, as well as the answer pages, to progress on their own. The answers are on pages 155 and 156.

Extensions

■ Invite students to write compound-complex sentences, using themselves as the subject.

■ Provide newspapers and magazines, and ask students to find and cut out examples of compound-complex sentences in the text. These cutout sentences may be used to create new news stories as well.

Student Study Page

Compound-Complex Sentences

A **compound-complex sentence** is made up of two or more independent clauses and one or more dependent clauses. The only difference between a compound-complex sentence and a complex sentence is that **a compound-complex sentence has two or more independent clauses.** For example:

> Even though he is my best friend, I will not allow him to insult you, and I will not put up with his bad manners.

> When my sister Ally looks at you with her big eyes, you always give her what she wants, and you enjoy doing it.

Each of these sentences has two independent clauses and one dependent clause. In the first example, the independent clauses are *I will not allow him to insult you* and *I will not put up with his bad manners;* the dependent clause is *Even though he is my best friend.* In the second example, the independent clauses are *you always give her what she wants* and *you enjoy doing it;* the dependent clause is *When my sister Ally looks at you with her big eyes.*

Name_____

Practice 1

Directions: Write an *S* in front of the simple sentences, a *C* in front of the compound sentences, an *X* in front of the complex sentences, and a *CC* in front of the compound-complex sentences.

_____ 1. Even though she is my best friend, I will not lie for her.

_____ 2. I was very upset when I heard what she had done; however, I understood her motives.

_____ 3. My parents forbid me to speak to her.

_____ 4. I didn't know what I should do.

_____ 5. I told my parents that I would speak to her because I felt that I should.

_____ 6. My parents respect my decision and trust me.

_____ 7. I was very embarrassed when I went to visit her.

_____ 8. She was happy to see me, and she greeted me as if nothing had happened.

_____ 9. I could see that she hadn't been sleeping very well.

_____ 10. I felt guilty about staying a short while, but I couldn't wait to leave.

106

Name_____

Practice 2

Directions: Choose the group of words that makes each sentence compound-complex. Write the sentence in the space below.

1. The players were (a) upset that they lost the game; (b) upset that they were losing and gave up; (c) upset that they were losing, but they didn't give up.

_____

_____

2. I believe (a) in you, and I always will; (b) that he has gone too far, and he will have to pay; (c) that he is an honest and kind man.

_____

_____

3. My sister won (a) first prize in the contest because she is so pretty; (b) a new car and a boat, but she is too young to drive; (c) a lot of prizes that she gave away, but she kept the biggest one.

_____

_____

4. No one wanted (a) the poor little cat, so I took it home with me; (b) the poor little cat except me, so I took it home, and I gave it to my sister as a present; (c) the poor little cat except me, but my mother said that I couldn't keep it.

_____

_____

5. The mysterious-looking man (a) followed me home, and then he tried to talk to me; (b) called my name, and then he slowly came toward me, but I was so frightened that I started to run; (c) approached me very cautiously, and then he put out his hand to get my attention.

_____

_____

Name_____

Practice 3

Directions: Choose the group of words that makes each sentence a compound-complex sentence. Write the sentence in the space below.

1. The truck was (a) going so fast that it went out of control, and it crashed; (b) a very large one that was carrying produce; (c) going very fast because it was behind schedule on its run.

   _____

   _____

2. Most people try (a) lots of things in their lifetime; (b) hard because they want to succeed; (c) different things because they like variety, but I don't.

   _____

   _____

3. The home was (a) antiseptically clean, and you could tell that no children had ever lived there; (b) warm and cozy, so we immediately felt at home; (c) not what I expected.

   _____

   _____

4. The escaped prisoner saw (a) a car, so he crept behind a large bush; (b) a group of people walking toward him just as he was getting ready to move on; (c) three police officers, and they had dogs with them that they used for tracking down escaped prisoners.

   _____

   _____

5. The comedy was (a) not really a comedy but a tearjerker; (b) very funny, and we laughed so hard that our sides ached; (c) not too funny because the main person dies.

   _____

   _____

Name_____

Practice 4

Directions: Here are groups of sentences. Combine each set of sentences into one compound-complex sentence. Write the sentence in the space below.

1. The game was almost over.
   Our team had still not scored.
   We still had hope.

   _____

   _____

2. The coach called for a time-out.
   He wanted to talk to the players.
   He wanted to build up their confidence.

   _____

   _____

3. The coach didn't yell at the team.
   He didn't criticize them either.
   He did give the players some sound advice.
   That's what they needed.

   _____

   _____

4. The players went back on the field.
   They looked refreshed.
   They looked stronger.

   _____

   _____

5. The play was called.
   Our team was ready.
   They made the point.

   _____

   _____

Name_____

Practice 5

Directions: Here are groups of sentences. Combine each set of sentences into one compound-complex sentence. Write the sentence in the space below.

1. I'm trying to be a neater person.
   It's very difficult.
   My stuff seems to be all over the place.

   _____

   _____

2. I need to finish cleaning my room.
   I cannot go outside.
   My friends are constantly asking me to come play.

   _____

   _____

3. I need to make an effort to be neat.
   I haven't been able to.
   I start to think about other things I would rather do.

   _____

   _____

4. My best friend is very busy.
   She always cleans up after herself.
   She is very neat.
   She likes things in their proper place.

   _____

   _____

5. The characters in some television shows seem busy all the time.
   They never seem to make a big mess.
   They are always neat and organized.

   _____

   _____

Name _____

Practice 6

Directions: Write five compound-complex sentences.

1. _____

_____

_____

2. _____

_____

_____

3. _____

_____

_____

4. _____

_____

_____

5. _____

_____

_____

SENTENCE EXPANSION USING MODIFIERS

Explanation

Sentences can be expanded or enlarged by adding words that modify (describe or limit) nouns and verbs. The descriptive words that modify nouns or pronouns are called **adjectives.** The descriptive words that modify verbs are called **adverbs.** Adverbs can also describe or limit an adjective or another adverb.

Modifiers (words that describe or limit another word or group of words) can consist of phrases or dependent clauses.

> Alfie is a dog that never barks or bothers anyone.
> A pen that doesn't write is useless.
> The man whose genius was acknowledged couldn't balance his own checkbook.

In the first example, the dependent clause *that never barks or bothers anyone* describes Alfie. In the second example, the dependent clause *that doesn't write* limits the word *pen* to a particular pen. In the last example, the dependent clause *whose genius was acknowledged* limits the word *man* to a particular man.

> The students in the play missed too many classes.
> She majored in economics.
> We attended for her benefit.

In the first example, the phrase *in the play* limits the word *students* to particular students. In the second example, the phrase *in economics* describes the verb *majored.* It tells in what she majored. In the last example, the phrase *for her benefit* describes the word *attended.* It tells why we attended.

Commas are used to set off modifiers that give additional information in a sentence or such information that is not necessary to the meaning of the sentence. In other words, if the additional information were omitted from the sentence, the omission would not change the meaning of the sentence or deprive the sentence of sense. Modifiers that give additional unrequired information are called **nonrestrictive modifiers.** For example:

> We visited England, my parents' birthplace, to learn more about our heritage.
> My old hat, which is faded and frayed, is my favorite.
> The long, tiring train ride, which seemed never to end, terminated in disaster for three people aboard.
> Maria, my best friend, is my maid of honor.

In these sentences, the information *parents' birthplace, which is faded and frayed, which seemed never to end,* and *my best friend,* is not necessary for the meaning of the sentences. These groups of words can be omitted because they are merely giving additional information. Therefore the group of words should be set off by commas.

Commas are not used to set off modifiers that give essential information that is necessary for the meaning of the sentence. If the essential information were omitted, the meaning or sense of the sentence would be changed. Modifiers that give necessary information are called **restrictive modifiers.**

> People who are secret agents must be especially trained for their jobs.
> The man who looks a little sheepish is the one who threw the lighted match in the wastebasket.
> The author Samuel Clemens wrote many books under the pseudonym of Mark Twain.

In these sentences, the information *who are secret agents, who looks a little sheepish,* and *Samuel Clemens,* is necessary for the meaning of the sentences. If these groups of words were omitted, the meanings of the sentences would change. In the first example, *who are secret agents* identifies those people to be especially trained. *Who are secret agents* limits the word *people* to a specific group. In the second example, *who looks a little sheepish* identifies the man who threw the lighted cigarette in the wastebasket. *Who looks a little sheepish* limits the word *man* to a specific person. In the third example, because *Samuel Clemens* limits the author to a specific one, it is essential information and requires no commas.

Special Note

In the sentence *Melissa, my friend, is very pretty,* the phrase *my friend* is set off with commas because it is additional information. However, in the sentence *My friend Melissa is very pretty,* the word *Melissa* is not set off with commas because *Melissa* limits or restricts the noun *friend. Melissa* tells you which friend is very pretty.

Learning Objectives

Your students should be able to:

- Add descriptive words to nouns and verbs.
- Expand a skeleton sentence using descriptive words.

Directions for Student Study Page and Practices

Use the student pages (pages 115–117) to help students acquire, reinforce, and review sentence expansion using modifiers. Reproduce the Student Study Page on page 115 for each student. This section can be used for reference while students do the student practices, as well as when they do their own writing.

Pick and choose the practices based on the needs and developmental levels of your students. Answers for the practice pages are reproducible, so you may choose to give your students the practice pages, as well as the answer pages to progress on their own. The answers are on pages 156 and 157.

Special Note

The teacher section contains information about restrictive and nonrestrictive modifiers that is not presented in the student section. Teachers should decide based on the individual differences of their students if and when they would want to introduce information on these more advanced concepts.

Extensions

- Divide the group into two teams. Encourage each team to come up with as many adjectives that are synonyms for the word *beautiful* as they can in a designated amount of time. The team with the most words wins. You may use other words such as *angry, tired, smart,* and so on.

- Give teams the word *cat.* Have them come up with as many adjectives that they can to describe a cat. Do the same for other nouns.

- Explain to students that newspaper reports most often are concise and to the point, using very few adjectives or adverbs. Provide newspapers and invite each student to choose a news story. Then challenge students to add adjectives and adverbs to enhance the stories. Encourage them to share their news stories with the rest of the group.

- Play a free association game. Name something and ask students to tell you what adjectives or adverbs they think of right away. Write these on the board as students say them. Continue with other nouns or verbs.

Student Study Page

Sentence Expansion Using Modifiers

Sentences can be expanded or enlarged by adding words that modify (describe or limit) nouns and verbs. The descriptive words that modify nouns or pronouns are called **adjectives.**

> The *silly old* cat meowed and meowed.
> I gave her a *big red* ball for a present.

The descriptive words that modify verbs are called **adverbs.** Adverbs can also describe or limit an adjective or another adverb. Adverbs generally tell how, when, where, or how much.

> The show started early. (when)
> He stood quietly. (how)
> She is very happy. (The word *very* describes the adjective *happy.*)
> They tried very hard. (The word *very* describes the adverb *hard.*)

The more descriptive words that are used in a sentence, the less general and more specific the sentence becomes. For example, let's expand the sentence *The cat runs.*

> The cat runs.
> The small, shaggy white cat runs swiftly.

The second sentence provides us much more information about the cat and its manner of running. Because the cat is small, shaggy, and white, all large, well-groomed, and other shades of cats are eliminated. The words *small, shaggy,* and *white* are called **modifiers.**

Special Note

Usually commas are not placed before descriptive words that refer to size, color, or age. For example: *cute little child; big brown dog; little old lady.*

Name _____

Practice 1

Directions: Fill in each blank with an adjective or adverb that gives more information about the noun or verb.

1. After the _____, _____ cheerleaders entered, everyone

   started cheering _____.

2. The _____ _____ students were sent _____

   to the doctor.

3. My _____ friend speaks _____.

4. The _____ _____ cat meowed _____.

5. _____ Jennifer laughs _____.

6. A(n) _____ _____ man dressed in _____

   _____ pants and a(n) _____ _____ shirt

   yelled _____ for the police.

7. The _____ _____ lady and the _____

   _____ man ran _____ down the _____

   street.

116

Name_____

Practice 2

Directions: Here are five sentences. Each is a "skeleton" sentence because it does not have any words that modify nouns or verbs. Expand each sentence using adjectives and adverbs. **Note:** The words *the* and *a* are being used in the sentences below, even though they are modifiers.

1. The cat drinks milk.

_____

_____

2. The team lost the game.

_____

_____

3. I read the child a story.

_____

_____

4. John answered the phone.

_____

_____

5. Jerry told Jennifer the news.

_____

_____

COMBINING SENTENCES

Explanation

In this book, your students have had practice in combining sentences. The exercises in this section provide students with more practice in this most important skill. Here are some pointers on sentence combining.

When writing sentences, you must decide which ideas are more important and which are less important. The less important ideas are subordinate to (dependent on) the more important ones. Your more important ideas are presented in independent or principal clauses, and your less important ideas are presented in subordinate or dependent clauses. Subordinate ideas are often introduced by such words as *although, as, because, since, until,* and *after.*

If the ideas you wish to present are of equal importance, then you will have two or more independent clauses, using coordinate conjunctions such as *and, but, or* or *for* to link your clauses. (See "Compound Sentences" on page 72.)

There are many ways to express the same or nearly the same idea. Or you can determine the exact meaning that you want. However, you should try to present ideas as clearly as possible. Knowledge of parallel construction helps you do this. Let's combine the following three sentences:

> Students enjoy dances.
> Students enjoy parties.
> Students enjoy concerts.
>
> Students enjoy dances, parties, and concerts.

This combined sentence has **parallel construction.** By this we mean that the elements that have been combined are all identical in structure; nouns should be joined only with nouns, adjectives only with adjectives, adverbs only with adverbs. In the example, the nouns *dances, parties,* and *concerts* are linked together with the coordinate conjunction *and.* Parallel construction may involve a series of words, such as nouns, verbs, adjectives, or adverbs, or a series of clauses or phrases.

The **coordinating conjunctions** (linking words that show an equal relation between or among things) such as *and, but,* and *or,* as well as the **correlative conjunctions** (linking words that show a one-to-one necessary relation between two sets of things), such as *either . . . or, neither . . . nor, not only, not only . . . but also, on one hand . . . on the other hand,* and *the one . . . the other,* are used in constructing parallel sentences.

Following are examples of sentences with parallel construction. Notice how you can show differences and similarities with such sentences.

The men *worked hard, laughed hard,* and *played hard.*

I can eat neither *fatty foods* nor *sweets.*

I feel *that college is worthwhile, that it helps you meet many people, that it prepares you for a profession,* and *that it helps you gain a broader education.*

She said that she would go to either *France* or *Spain* this summer.

Scuba diving is *dangerous* and *costly* but *thrilling.*

The police looked for the criminal *in the vacant house, in the swampland,* and *in the woods beyond the swampland.*

He said *that he would help me with my problem* but *that he would not tell me what to do.*

The following are examples of the various ways sentences can be combined or joined together.

1. Jack is athletic. Jack is intelligent.

   Jack is athletic and intelligent. (simple sentence)

2. Tony likes rock music. Tony likes classical music.

   (a) Tony likes rock and classical music. (simple sentence)

   (b) Although Tony likes rock music, he also likes classical music. (complex sentence)

3. I studied astronomy. I studied physiology. I studied geology.

   I studied astronomy, physiology, and geology. (simple sentence)

4. The deer fled from the hunters. The hunters continued to pursue them.

   The deer fled from the hunters, but the hunters continued to pursue them. (compound sentence)

5. The finals were very difficult.
   We passed all of them.

   (a) Although the finals were very difficult. We passed all of them. (complex sentence)

   (b) The finals were very difficult, but we passed all of them. (compound sentence)

   (c) Although we passed all of them, the finals were very difficult. (complex sentence)

   (d) The finals were very difficult; nevertheless, we passed all of them. (compound sentence)

6. Jim came to school on crutches.
   He had a broken leg.

   (a) Jim came to school on crutches because he had a broken leg. (complex sentence)

   (b) Although he had a broken leg, Jim came to school on crutches. (complex sentence)

   (c) Jim came to school on crutches when he had a broken leg. (complex sentence)

7. Anthony developed laryngitis on the night of our big debate. Anthony is our best debater.

   (a) Anthony, our best debater, developed laryngitis on the night of the big debate. (simple sentence)

   (b) Anthony, who is our best debater, developed laryngitis on the night of the big debate. (complex sentence)

8. Jack is a hunter. His brother, Herb, is a trapper. They both went to pursue the elusive Big Foot.

   (a) Jack, a hunter, and his brother, Herb, a trapper, went to pursue the elusive Big Foot. (simple sentence)

   (b) Jack, who is a hunter, and his brother, Herb, who is a trapper, went to pursue the elusive Big Foot. (complex sentence)

9. We went shopping.
   We went to a movie.
   We went out to supper.

   (a) We went shopping, to a movie, and out to supper. (simple sentence)

   (b) First we went shopping and to a movie, and then we went out to supper. (compound sentence)

   (c) After we went shopping and to a movie, we went out to supper. (complex sentence)

10. The man is sitting over there. He is unhappy. He is depressed. He is looking for a job. He can't find one.

(a) The unhappy, depressed man who is sitting over there is looking for a job, but he can't find one. (compound-complex sentence)

(b) The man sitting over there is unhappy and depressed because he is looking for a job, but he can't find one. (compound-complex sentence)

Special Note

Any sentence that uses coordinating conjunctions is a parallel sentence. However, the most common parallel sentences consist of a series (a group of usually three or more things or events) of nouns, verbs, adjectives, adverbs, phrases, or clauses.

Learning Objectives

Your students should be able to:

- Combine each set of sentences into one sentence.
- Combine each set of sentences in at least two different ways.

Directions for Student Study Pages and Practices

Use the student pages (pages 122–130) to help students acquire, reinforce, and review combining sentences. Reproduce the Student Study Pages on pages 122–125 for each student. This section can be used for reference while students do the practices, as well as when they do their own writing.

Pick and choose the practices based on the needs and developmental levels of your students. Answers for the practice pages are reproducible, so you may choose to give your students the practice pages, as well as the answer pages, to progress on their own. The answers are on pages 157 and 158.

Extensions

- Print out a number of sentences on heavy paper or poster board. Cut out each sentence and invite students to combine as many sentences that make sense as they can. You may want to divide the group into teams and have each team create as many sentences as they can in a specific amount of time.

- Give each student a page from the newspaper and ask them to cut out as many different types of sentences that they can find in the text. Students can then combine the cutout sentences to make up interesting news items.

Name _____

Student Study Pages

Combining Sentences

You have been learning to combine sentences. This section will give you more practice in sentence combining.

Good writers often balance their simple sentences with longer and more involved ones. When writing sentences, you must decide which ideas are more important and which are less important. The less important ideas are dependent on the more important ideas. **Your more important ideas are presented in your principal or independent clause, and your less important ideas are presented in your dependent clause.** Dependent clauses are often introduced by such words as *although, as, because, if, since, until,* and *after.* For example:

John went to the party *because* everyone else was going.

If the ideas you wish to present are of equal importance, then you will have two or more independent clauses. You can combine independent clauses with such coordinate (equal) conjunctions as *and, but, or,* or *for.* For example:

Susan needs help, *but* she will not ask for it.

The following are three examples of sentence combining.

1. Sarita is happy.
   Camile is happy.
   Charlie is happy.

   Sarita, Camile, and Charlie are happy.
   (simple sentence)

2. My sister made the basketball team.
   My brother did not make the football team.

   My sister made the basketball team, but my brother did not
   make the football team.
   (compound sentence)

Student Study Pages *continued*

3. My brother does well in school.
He doesn't study very much.

My brother does well in school, even though he doesn't study very much. (complex sentence)

A comma is usually used before a coordinate conjunction, such as *and, but, for, or,* and *nor,* when the coordinate conjunction joins independent clauses to form a compound sentence.

I like to swim, and my sister likes to jog.
My best friend told us not to buy him a present for his birthday,
but no one listened to him.

When linking words such as *however, therefore, then,* and *also* join two independent clauses to form a compound sentence, a semicolon is usually used before the linking word.

The game ended at 5:00 p.m. on Tuesday; then every one of us went
out for an ice cream soda.
Last week my friends and I toured a haunted house; however,
it didn't frighten us.

A comma is usually used after a dependent clause when it comes before an independent clause in a complex sentence.

When my cousins visit on Saturday, we usually go to a movie.
Although she gets the best grades in class, she is not a show-off.

The following are examples of the various ways sentences can be combined or joined together.

1. Jack is athletic. Jack is intelligent.

    Jack is athletic and intelligent.
       (simple sentence)

2. Tony likes rock music. Tony likes classical music.

    (a) Tony likes rock and classical music.
        (simple sentence)

    (b) Although Tony likes rock music,
        he also likes classical music.
        (complex sentence)

Student Study Pages *continued*

3. I studied civics. I studied geometry. I studied algebra.

   I studied civics, geometry, and algebra. (simple sentence)

4. The deer fled from the hunters. The hunters continued to pursue them.

   The deer fled from the hunters, but the hunters continued to pursue them. (compound sentence)

5. The finals were very difficult. We passed all of them.

   (a) Although the finals were very difficult, we passed all of them. (complex sentence)

   (b) The finals were very difficult, but we passed all of them. (compound sentence)

   (c) Although we passed all of them, the finals were very difficult. (complex sentence)

   (d) The finals were very difficult; nevertheless, we passed all of them. (compound sentence)

6. Jim came to school on crutches. He had a broken leg.

   (a) Jim came to school on crutches because he had a broken leg. (complex sentence)

   (b) Although he had a broken leg, Jim came to school on crutches. (complex sentence)

   (c) Jim came to school on crutches when he had a broken leg. (complex sentence)

7. Michael developed laryngitis on the night of our big debate. Michael is our best debater.

   (a) Michael, our best debater, developed laryngitis on the night of our big debate. (simple sentence)

   (b) Michael, who is our best debater, developed laryngitis on the night of the big debate. (complex sentence)

Student Study Pages *continued*

8. Jack is a hunter. His brother, Herb, is a trapper. They both went to pursue the elusive Big Foot.

   (a) Jack, a hunter, and his brother, Herb, a trapper, went to pursue the elusive Big Foot. (simple sentence)

   (b) Jack, who is a hunter, and his brother, Herb, who is a trapper, went to pursue the elusive Big Foot. (complex sentence)

9. We went shopping. We went to a movie. We went out to supper.

   (a) We went shopping, to a movie, and out to supper. (simple sentence)

   (b) First we went shopping and to a movie, and then we went out to supper. (compound sentence)

   (c) After we went shopping and to a movie, we went out to supper. (complex sentence)

10. The young man is sitting over there. He is unhappy. He is depressed. He is looking for a job after school. He can't find one.

   (a) The unhappy, depressed young man who is sitting over there is looking for a job after school, but he can't find one. (compound-complex sentence)

   (b) The young man sitting over there is unhappy and depressed because he is looking for a job after school, but he can't find one. (compound-complex sentence)

Name_____

Practice 1

Directions: Combine each set of sentences into one sentence. Write the sentence in the space below.

Example: Sally is my best friend. She's fun to be with.

Sally is my best friend because she is fun to be with.

OR

Sally is my best friend, and she's fun to be with.

1. Jonathan is funny. He likes to laugh a lot.

   _____

   _____

2. Alisa wants to be a cheerleader. Julie wants to be a cheerleader.

   _____

   _____

3. Every morning Jeff rides his bike to school. Every morning Lisa rides her bike to school. Every morning Kim rides her bike to school.

   _____

   _____

4. Lee is trying out for a part in the play. Anna is trying out for a part in the play. Terry is trying out for a part in the play. Jason is not trying out for a part in the play. Rachel is not trying out for a part in the play.

   _____

   _____

5. The story is a horror tale. It frightens me. It gives me nightmares.

   _____

   _____

Name _____

Practice 2

Directions: Combine each set of sentences into one sentence. Write the sentence in the space below.

Example: Jim and Judy are trying out for the play. They will not get parts in it.

Although Jim and Judy are trying out for the play, they will not
get parts in it.

OR

Jim and Judy are trying out for the play, but they will not get parts in it.

1. Mary is happy. Dave is happy. Sondra is happy.

_____

_____

2. Jakeel is good in sports. His brother is not.

_____

_____

3. My friend's father is an engineer. His mother is a scientist. His brother is a forest ranger.

_____

_____

4. Benita started to work on her paper. She got tired. She went to sleep.

_____

_____

5. My cat's name is Feather. Feather is small. Feather is white. Feather is soft. Feather will only drink out of her own dish.

_____

_____

Name _____

Practice 3

Directions: Here are three sets of sentences. Combine each set in at least two different ways. Write the sentence in the space below.

1. My sister is captain of the basketball team. She is very tall. She is athletic.

_____

_____

_____

_____

_____

2. Gary shouldn't go horseback riding. Gary is allergic to horses. Gary sneezes a lot. Gary loves to go horseback riding.

_____

_____

_____

_____

_____

3. The farmers were angry. Wild dogs were eating their chickens. The farmers called a meeting. They decided to hunt down the wild dogs.

_____

_____

_____

_____

_____

Name _____

Practice 4

Directions: Here are three sets of sentences. Combine each set in at least two different ways. Write the sentence in the space below.

1. Jennifer baby-sits. Jennifer loves children. Jennifer doesn't need the money.

_____

_____

_____

_____

_____

2. The boy is running. The people are running after him. The boy keeps looking over his shoulder. The people look angry.

_____

_____

_____

_____

_____

3. Tomorrow is the championship game. Our star player is ill. We are trying to postpone the game. We can't.

_____

_____

_____

_____

_____

Name_____

Practice 5

Directions: Combine each set of sentences into one sentence. The sentences may be simple, compound, complex, or compound-complex. Write the sentence in the space below.

1. The girl is pretty. The girl is young. The girl goes into a store.

   _____

   _____

2. My garden is filled with a variety of flowers. My garden has roses. My garden has lilies of the valley. My garden has daisies.

   _____

   _____

3. A man is walking slowly down the street. The man is wearing a dark suit. The man is carrying a briefcase.

   _____

   _____

4. A sailor is walking quickly toward the diner. The sailor has a patch over one eye. The sailor is limping.

   _____

   _____

5. A whistle blew. People started to come out of their houses. The people wanted to see what was happening.

   _____

   _____

6. The man is middle-aged. The man is frightened. The man is carrying a package. The man sees two men. The two men are following him. The man starts to run.

   _____

   _____

Student's Name _____

Assessment Tool Progress Report

Progress

_____

_____

_____

_____

_____

Improvement

_____

_____

_____

_____

_____

Comments

_____

_____

_____

_____

_____

Name _____

Posttest for Writing and Thinking Skills

Capitalization and Punctuation

Directions: Rewrite each sentence correctly using the proper punctuation.

1. dr d chow asked whether we could meet at 5:00 pm

   _____

2. my mother said i could invite my friends to my halloween party in october

   _____

3. we will move from stuart rd to hardy ave on june 5 2001

   _____

4. lee is going to visit mr and mrs jones on january 5 2001

   _____

5. who is going to leslies party on sunday

   _____

Punctuation

Directions: Put the proper punctuation at the end of each sentence.

1. Kristin asked whether the story was funny
2. Look out
3. Who yelled so loudly
4. Rodriguez did very well on the test
5. Is Ally your best friend

Direct Quotations

Directions: Put in the correct punctuation to make these direct quotations correct.

1. Rueben asked why are you so upset
2. Stacy said I need more time to finish all that homework
3. Esteban said there is not enough time to do everything
4. Mohammed asked what can I do to help
5. Sara said speak to the teacher

Direct and Indirect Quotations

Directions: The following sentences contain indirect quotations. Rewrite each sentence so that it contains a direct quotation.

1. The twins said that they want to go rollerblading.

_____

2. We told them that we have to do homework.

_____

3. Rasheed said that he could go after he practices the piano.

_____

4. Molly said that she has dance class after school.

_____

5. Lee said that he had to play soccer after school.

_____

Contractions

Directions: Write the contractions for the following.

1. there is _____ 　　6. who is _____

2. he is _____ 　　7. where is _____

3. they will _____ 　　8. what is _____

4. it is _____ 　　9. will not _____

5. let us _____ 　　10. has not _____

Posttest for Writing and Thinking Skills *continued*

Commas

Directions: Each of the following sentences has two adjectives. Add commas between adjectives where needed. If a sentence does not need a comma, write *NC* in the blank.

1. Sara's pretty red shoes look good on her feet. _____

2. That is a large scary-looking dog. _____

3. What beautiful long hair you have. _____

4. I cannot eat that hot spicy food. _____

5. My itchy sore arm hurts. _____

Recognizing Sentences

Directions: Underline each group of words that is a sentence.

1. Everyone is coming to my party.

2. In the large room.

3. While you wait here for them.

4. Who said that I would go?

5. After all that time.

Word Order in Sentences

Directions: Use the following groups of words to write sentences. Include the necessary commas.

1. Stitch time a nine in saves.

   _____

2. Milk is use there no over spilled crying.

   _____

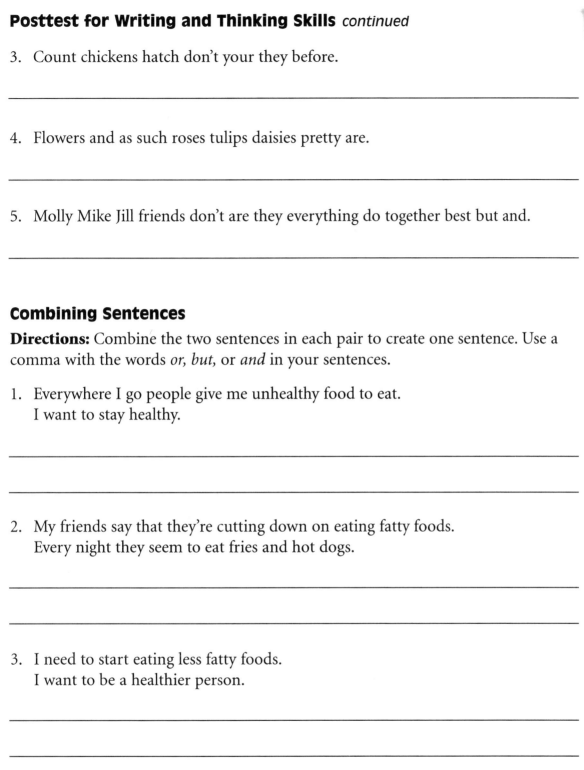

3. Count chickens hatch don't your they before.

_____

4. Flowers and as such roses tulips daisies pretty are.

_____

5. Molly Mike Jill friends don't are they everything do together best but and.

_____

_____

Combining Sentences

Directions: Combine the two sentences in each pair to create one sentence. Use a comma with the words *or, but,* or *and* in your sentences.

1. Everywhere I go people give me unhealthy food to eat.
   I want to stay healthy.

_____

_____

2. My friends say that they're cutting down on eating fatty foods.
   Every night they seem to eat fries and hot dogs.

_____

_____

3. I need to start eating less fatty foods.
   I want to be a healthier person.

_____

_____

4. I am doing more exercises.
   It's paying off.

_____

_____

5. My friends know what they should eat.
    They still eat lots of junk food.

_____

_____

Shortening Sentences

Directions: Shorten the following sentences using commas. Write the sentence in the space below.

1. Marisa likes to run every day. Fred likes to run every day. Molly likes to run every day.

_____

2. Kelly loves to eat Chinese food and Mexican food and Italian food and French food.

_____

3. Roberto and Peggy and Kaitlin and Kathy are all good friends.

_____

4. We are going to a movie tomorrow and we are going to a museum tomorrow and we are going to a party tomorrow.

_____

_____

5. Julie is playing soccer today and Florenzio is playing soccer today and Rashmid is playing soccer today and Corrie is playing soccer today and Lee is playing soccer today.

_____

_____

Independent and Dependent Clauses

Directions: Underline the dependent clause in each sentence.

1. Kristin is doing very well because she is a hard worker.

2. When Molly is tired, she stops working.

3. I eat ice cream, even though it is cold outside.

4. The doctor put Tracy in the hospital when she had a very high fever.

5. Bill got a stomachache because he ate too much.

Combining Independent and Dependent Clauses

Directions: Combine the two sentences in each of the following pairs. Use one of the linking words listed below, and add necessary commas. Write the sentence in the space below.

   although, because, even though, if, when

1. My friends go rollerblading every Friday.
   It is fun.

   _____

   _____

2. We refused to go indoors.
   It was snowing.

   _____

   _____

3. They can get the supplies they need.
   They go shopping.

   _____

   _____

4. Two of my friends walked into a tree.
   They weren't looking where they were going.

   _____

   _____

5. Perez did very well on his exams.
   He does his homework every day.

   _____

   _____

Adjectives and Adverbs

Directions: Fill in each blank with the correct adjective or adverb.

1. The _____ clown ran _____ than the children.
   (silly, sillier, faster)

2. The _____ poem was read _____ by Jacob.
   (better, best, beautifully)

3. Molly plays chess _____ than her brother, but he plays checkers

   the _____ of everyone.
      (well, best, better)

4. The _____ children _____ ran outside.
   (patiently, impatient, quickly)

5. My _____ friend always arrives at parties the _____.
   (early, best, earliest)

Posttest for Writing and Thinking Skills

Student Progress Assessment Record

Count how many items you answered correctly in the Posttest. Write your score in the *My Score* column. Look at the score in the *Good Score* column. If your score is as high as the good score, you are ready to continue with more writing and thinking skills. If your score on the test falls below the good score, restudy the material for that particular test.

	Good Score	My Score
Capitalizing and Punctuation	4–5 (no errors in sentence)	
Punctuation	4–5 (no errors in sentence)	
Direct Quotations	4–5 (no errors in sentence)	
Direct and Indirect Quotations	4–5 (no errors in sentence)	
Contractions	9–0	
Commas	4–5	
Recognizing Sentences	5	
Word Order in Sentences	4–5	
Combining Sentences	4–5	
Shortening Sentences	4–5	
Independent and Dependent Clauses	5	
Combining Independent and Dependent Clauses	5	
Adjectives and Adverbs	5	

Diagnostic Checklist for General and Practical Aspects of Writing

Student's Name _____

Grade _____

Teacher _____

Capitalization	Yes	No	Sometimes
The student capitalizes:			
1. persons' names.			
2. the first word of a sentence.			
3. the greeting in a letter.			
4. days of the week.			
5. months of the year.			
6. titles of persons, such as *Mr., Mrs., Miss,* and *Ms.*			
7. the first word of the closing of a letter.			
8. names of states.			
9. names of cities.			
10. names of streets.			
11. the pronoun *I*.			
12. the first word of every line in a poem (with some exceptions).			
13. names of countries.			
14. names of towns.			
15. names of avenues.			
16. names of roads.			
17. any word used as a name, such as *Father* or *Mother*.			
18. titles of books.			

The student capitalizes:	Yes	No	Sometimes
19. titles of poems.			
20. titles of stories.			
21. titles of movies.			
22. titles of magazines.			
23. names of languages.			
24. names of buildings.			
25. names of companies.			
26. the first word of a direct quotation.			
27. names of institutions.			
28. historical periods.			
29. names of nationalities.			
30. directions that name definite areas.			
31. in outlining, the first word of each main topic, subtopic, and detail.			

Punctuation	Yes	No	Sometimes
The student:			
1. places periods at the end of sentences.			
2. places periods after abbreviations.			
3. places question marks at the end of question sentences.			
4. uses commas to separate day from year (February 11, 1980).			
5. uses commas to separate city from state (Albany, New York).			
6. places periods after numbers in a listing (1. candy, 2. cake, and so on).			

The student:	Yes	No	Sometimes
7. places periods after *Mr., Mrs.,* and *Ms.*			
8. places periods after initials (J. Jones, C.S. Lewis, and so on).			
9. uses apostrophes in some contractions such as *can't* and *he's.*			
10. uses apostrophes in singular possessives such as *girl's* and *boy's.*			
11. uses apostrophes in more contractions such as *let us/let's* and *will not/won't.*			
12. uses apostrophes in singular and plural possessives, such as *Jones's, Joneses, children's, babies',* and *mice's.*			
13. uses hyphens between syllables in separating words at the end of lines.			
14. uses exclamation points to express strong emphasis or emotion.			
15. uses exclamation points for commands (optional).			
16. uses commas to separate items in a series.			
17. uses colons after salutations in business letters.			
18. uses commas to set off quotations.			
19. places quotation marks before and after quotations.			
20. uses commas to help make sentences clearer.			
21. uses commas in numbers with more than four digits (optional for four-digit numbers).			
22. uses commas with transitional words such as *however, indeed, that is, for example,* and *in fact.*			

The student:	Yes	No	Sometimes
23. uses quotation marks for special words in sentences.			
24. uses quotation marks for setting off titles of poems, short stories, magazine articles, chapters, and so on.			
25. uses colons to set off lists of items.			
26. underlines titles of books.			
27. uses a comma before a linking word, such as *and* or *but,* when the linking word joins two simple sentences to form a compound sentence.			
28. uses a semicolon before a linking word, such as *however* or *therefore,* when the linking word joins two simple sentences to form a compound sentence.			

Sentences

The student:	Yes	No	Sometimes
1. writes simple sentences in the active voice.			
2. recognizes that sentence fragments are not sentences.			
3. recognizes that a sentence expresses a complete thought.			
4. recognizes that a sentence may be as brief as one word, such as *Go!,* and that *you* is understood in such a sentence.			
5. writes statement sentences.			
6. writes question sentences.			
7. writes command sentences.			

Diagnostic Checklist for General and Practical Aspects of Writing *continued*

The student:	Yes	No	Sometimes
8. writes exclamatory sentences.			
9. expands sentences by adding descriptive words.			
10. combines sentences.			
11. recognizes run-on sentences.			
12. corrects run-on sentences.			
13. writes compound sentences.			
14. writes complex sentences.			
15. writes compound-complex sentences.			

Answers

Capitalization

Student Review for Capitalization (page 20)

1. Mr. and Mrs. J. S. Hill are the parents of Eric and Ilse.
2. In May, my brother and I are going to school in a small town in Texas.
3. In the summer, my parents and I are going to visit the Smithsonian Institution in Washington, D. C.
4. Kelsey, Melissa, Anna, and I are going to a party at the Perez's house on Warren Street in October.
5. My cousin, my sister, my aunt, and I will visit New York City the last Monday in June.

Capitalization Practices
Practice 1 (page 24)

1. My Aunt Sally came to visit us from Europe.
2. I do not do well in English.
3. Ms. Amad lives on Seventh Avenue in Minneapolis.
4. Our uncle lives in the South, and our grandparents live in the West.
5. In our history class, we are studying the Constitution of the United States.
6. No one knew that Mr. Brown wrote the poem "Life's Moments."
7. On Sunday, our school is having a picnic in the new part of town.
8. The football game was held in Davis Stadium on Saturday.
9. Ricardo, Sandy, Chuck, and Nate received a special award in January.
10. Rashid said, "Not even Alisa and I are going on Monday."

Practice 2 (page 25)

1. My father, mother, and Uncle Dave got lost on Tuesday in an old part of town.
2. I enjoy history, geography, and languages such as German and French.
3. On Sunday we usually go skating in the park, and then we go to a restaurant to eat.
4. Football and basketball are my favorite sports, but I'm better in chess than in either of the others.
5. When my cousin fell, we took him to the hospital.
6. In the summer, I usually go to camp with my brother.
7. When we traveled north last spring, I met a famous poet.
8. In the olden days, children used to recite verse, such as the following: "I was ever born in sin,/ And all my heart is bad within."
9. I enjoyed my trip west, but I was surprised that I did not see many actresses and actors in Hollywood.
10. The stewards on the ship told all the passengers to be calm, but it's difficult to be calm with Hurricane Diane raging over you.

Practice 3 (page 26)

1. My father is a doctor, and my mother is a lawyer.
2. The title of my poem is "The Trials of a Bug."
3. Spring and fall are the seasons I like the best.
4. When Rev. Jim Brown spoke, everyone in the audience listened.
5. My favorite aunt is Aunt Jane, and my favorite uncle is Uncle Peter.

Practice 4 (page 27)

1. Chrysler Building 2. *The Taming of the Shrew* 3. winter 4. Ms. Smith
5. C 6. C 7. Dr. Sarah Brown 8. C 9. Wednesday 10. C 11. I 12. the Joneses
13. a map 14. C 15. Egypt 16. Asia 17. Blanding Street 18. Aunt Sharon
19. cousin 20. *The Boy Who Could Make Himself Disappear*

Practice 5 (page 28)

(Sample Answers)

1. My friends Carol Smith and Sharon Johnson live in Memphis.
2. Dr. Brown gave a talk to our class on the first Monday of February.
3. *The Dream Watcher* by Wersba is a book I like because I can relate to the main character.
4. My favorite game is tennis, and my favorite subjects are history and English.
5. One of my favorite poems is "Birches" by Robert Frost.

Punctuation

Student Review for Punctuation (page 34)

1. a. couldn't b. won't c. didn't d. can't e. he's f. they're g. I'm h. she'll
   i. we're j. it's
2. a. Dear Rasheen, b. Sincerely yours, c. How old are you? d. I am eleven years
   old. e. Ms. f. Dr. g. Mr. h. Mrs. i. Help! **or** Help? j. Ave. k. C. A. Smith
   l. S. Jones
3. a. man's b. girl's c. book's d. class's e. student's f. apple's g. lady's h. boy's
   i. Dallas's j. watch's
4. a. April 1, 1999
   b. John St.
      Trenton, New Jersey 08625
   c. May 25, 1952
   d. J. J. Jackson
   e. K. S. Perry
      73 Cherry Ave.
      Manhasset Hills, New York 11040

Punctuation Practices
Practice 1 (page 40)

1. Who are you?
2. Don't go yet.
3. I need more time to do that.

Practice 1 (page 40) continued

4. When are you leaving?
5. That is fantastic!
6. We all passed our exams.
7. Henry refused to go to the party with us.
8. Imagine that!
9. Stop. **or** Stop!
10. Is he telling the truth?

Practice 2 (page 41)

(Sample Answers)

1. When is our test?
2. I have to read 50 pages for tomorrow's test.
3. Come here.
4. That is marvelous!
5. Stop that immediately!

Practice 3 (page 42)

1. O
2. O
3. Jack, Alicia, and Marta are not here.
4. Jim went swimming before breakfast, before lunch, and before dinner.
5. My favorite subjects are French, English, and geography.
6. Kayla is smart, pretty, and fun to be with.
7. My best friend is a member of the chorus, a member of the band, and a member of the debate club.
8. He is poor, tired, and sad.
9. O
10. The bell rang once, twice, and three times.

Practice 4 (page 43)

1. O
2. The bell rang very loudly, and then the children stopped playing.
3. I studied hard for the exam, but the material I studied wasn't on it.
4. My friend passed the exam, for she had studied the correct material.
5. I passed the exam, but I did not get a good grade on it.
6. Yesterday I studied for the wrong exam, and I had an argument with my friend.
7. The ride was scary, thrilling, and breathtaking.
8. I tried out for the football team, and my friend tried out for the basketball team.
9. The guys on the football team are strong, big, and athletic.
10. Our uniforms are green, white, and yellow.
11. After Jim left the room, people began to say mean things about him.
12. O

Practice 4 (page 43) continued

13. When my best friend started to poke fun at Jim, I became very upset.
14. Jill, Josh, Elise, and I left the party and went home.
15. When my big black dog greeted me at the door, I felt good.

Practice 5 (page 44)

1. My brother, sister, father, and mother are coming to visit my class.
2. I enjoy playing games, watching television, and reading.
3. Yesterday we swam, water-skied, and hiked.
4. The cat is cute, cuddly, and smart.
5. My friends Tyrel, Jim, and Jack are studying for history, math, and English tests.
6. My favorite flavors are vanilla, chocolate, and strawberry.

Practice 6 (page 45)

1. The train arrived two hours late, for it had engine trouble.
2. When my parents changed jobs, we had to move to another state.
3. Even though my brother is a star athlete, he is not a snob.
4. I never get away with anything; however, my sister always does.
5. My sister is a cheerleader; therefore, she gets to go to all the games.
6. I have to be home by a certain time, but my sister can stay out as late as she wants.
7. Art is my favorite subject, but I am a terrible artist.
8. The door opened slowly; then a huge hand came into view and turned out the lights.
9. After I saw my mistakes, I felt ill.
10. If I don't do better on the next exam, I won't be able to play in the big game.

Practice 7 (page 46)

1. O
2. "Chicago," "Birches," and "The Sea"
3. "Controlled Experiments in the Classroom,"
4. Britta said, "I learned some interesting things from my controlled experiment."
5. O
6. Marika said, "I need more paper."
7. Jake asked, "Why aren't we going on the plane yet?"
8. Ben said, "The plane is delayed because of a storm."
9. Our instructor asked, "Do you understand the question?"

Writing Simple Sentences

Student Review for Writing Simple Sentences (page 52)

1. My brother and his friend like to rollerblade. (2)
2. Kelsey runs very fast and jumps rope very well. (1)

Student Review for Writing Simple Sentences (page 52) continued

3. <u>Karem</u> is a good soccer player. (1)
4. <u>Lisa</u>, <u>Kristin</u>, <u>Bridget</u>, and <u>Anna</u> came to Melissa's birthday party. (2)
5. <u>Friends</u> are nice to have. (1)
6. The twins <u>ride</u> their bikes to school every day. (1)
7. Our teacher and principal <u>spoke</u> to us about the writing contest. (1)
8. The children <u>screamed</u> and <u>cried</u> all day. (2)
9. The pilot <u>flew</u> the plane above the clouds. (1)
10. We all <u>laughed</u> and <u>applauded</u> the pilot at the end of our trip. (2)

11–14 Answers will vary.
(Sample Answers)
11. (one subject and one verb) Maria plays with her friends.
12. (two subjects and one verb) Maria and Anna play nicely together.
13. (one subject and two verbs) Maria plays soccer and rollerblades.
14. (two subjects and two verbs) Maria and Anna ice-skate and ski together.

Writing Simple Sentences Practices*

*The answers given for most of these practices are sample answers. Students' answers will vary for open-ended practices.

Practice 1 (page 58)

Numbers 1, 2, 3, 5, 6, 7, and 8 are complete sentences.
Numbers 4, 9, and 10 are not sentences.
The rewritten sentences for 4, 9, and 10 will vary.

Practice 2 (page 59)

Many years ago, the great magician Merlin, looking; Like a beggar; Stopped at a peasant's cottage one evening; The wife brought out; Some fresh bread and milk for him; Being a magician; and *To reward them* are all sentence fragments.

Sample Sentences: Many years ago, the great magician Merlin, looking like a beggar, stopped at a peasant's cottage one evening. The wife brought out some fresh bread and milk for him. Being a magician, Merlin decided to reward them.

Practice 3 (page 60)

1. I ride a bike to school.
2. Help me.
3. Where do you live?
4. My friends are friendly and fun to be with.
5. The animals in the zoo do tricks.
6. The clown in the circus stood on his head.
7. I intend to be the driver in the race.
8. I intend to be in the Olympics.

Practice 3 (page 60) continued

9. No one knew what to do.
10. My allowance is always gone in two days.

Practice 4 (page 61)

1. Where are you going?
2. My best subject is reading. **or** Reading is my best subject.
3. Our basketball team won the game. **or** Our team won the basketball game.
4. We are having a party at my house.
5. Tomorrow we are leaving for the beach. **or** We are leaving for the beach tomorrow.
6. I have a lot of homework and a bad headache.
7. In two days my best friend is having a birthday party. **or** My best friend is having a birthday party in two days.
8. In the summer we are going to tour the United States. **or** We are going to tour the United States in the summer.

Practice 5 (page 62)

(Sample Combinations)

1. Craig is a new student in our class. (1. d)
2. They are not very friendly to him. (2. a)
3. No one ever chooses him for anything. (3. g)
4. The other students ignore him. (4. f)
5. I feel sorry for him. (5. b)
6. The teacher has tried to help him in class. (6. h)
7. Everyone makes fun of him. (7. j)
8. Which person will help him? (8. i)
9. He needs help. (9. e)
10. Life must be difficult for him. (10. c)

Practice 6 (page 63)

(Sample Answers)

1. After the game, John will go to the party.
2. Stop that!
3. She is a jolly person.
4. The dog turned a somersault.
5. Vanessa played for us.

Practice 7 (page 64)

Sentences will vary.

Practice 8 (page 65)

(Sample Answers)

1. They **or** Marcie and Peter
2. She **or** Tawanda

Practice 8 (page 65) continued

3. They **or** Tennis and swimming
4. brother
5. coat
6. report
7. Basketball
8. They **or** Pierre and Frank
9. you **or** they **or** Krista and Kayla
10. She **or** Peggy

Practice 9 (page 66)

(Sample Answers)

1. The bright red wound and the deep cut needed care immediately.
2. Susan and Tony fight a lot.
3. Richard plays baseball every day.
4. Jack and Sam like to do that.
5. Don, Susan, and Marie argue too much.

Practice 10 (page 67)

(Sample Combinations)

1. Slappy, the clown, and Slerpy, the dog, perform together. (1. d)
2. The mixed-up cat and the helpful mouse play together. (2. f)
3. The ferocious lion and its trainer thrill the audience. (3. g)
4. The dinosaur and the flying serpent no longer exist. (4. h)
5. Superman and Batman are comic book characters. (5. a)
6. Sun and water are needed for plants. (6. b)
7. The bus and train are common means of public transportation. (7. j)
8. Fruits and vegetables are the foods of vegetarians. (8. c)
9. The mongoose and the cobra are natural enemies. (9. e)
10. Raisins and prunes are dried fruits. (10. i)

Practice 11 (page 68)

(Sample Combinations)

1. The good fairy smiled and touched the child with her wand. (1. f)
2. Clever Gretel tricked the witch. (2. g)
3. The golden bird laughed and laid a golden egg. (3. d)
4. Rapunzel started to sing and let down her hair. (4. h)
5. The old woman in the woods ran after the girl and caught her. (5. b)
6. The little match girl waited for someone to buy her wares. (6. j)
7. The six swans dropped from the sky and flew about the queen. (7. a)
8. The three spinners entered, sat down, and began to spin. (8. i)
9. The six travelers entered and refreshed themselves. (9. c)
10. Jack the Giant Killer seized the trumpet and blew a great blast. (10. e)

ANSWERS

Practice 12 (page 69)

(Sample Sentences)

1. We work hard and play hard.
2. Machines break down and need repairs.
3. The peculiar bird sings and flies in circles.
4. Some people argue and fight all the time.
5. The cross-eyed animal stared at us and then charged.
6. A bowlegged duck waddled across the street and stopped traffic.
7. The clown laughed and cried.
8. The accused man laughed and sneered at the jurors.
9. The winner of the contest jumped up and down, clapped her hands, and shouted with joy.
10. The athlete practices every day, eats well, and gets plenty of fresh air and sleep.

Practice 13 (page 70)

(Sample Combinations)

1. A little girl and her godmother spin and weave for a living. (1. e)
2. The golden bird and the golden horse did not fly and did not run. (2. j)
3. The wicked brother and the fox met and fought. (3. f)
4. The king and queen greeted and kissed the princess. (4. g)
5. A sea captain and his friends were found and imprisoned. (5. a)
6. The dancing dog and the meowing cat run and play all day. (6. b)
7. The princess and her sister plucked and ate the forbidden apple. (7. d)
8. The princess and the miller boy got into the coach and rode away. (8. h)
9. Tom Thumb and the mouse played and had fun. (9. c)
10. A giant and a dwarf laughed and joked. (10. i)

Practice 14 (page 71)

Sentences will vary.

Compound Sentences

Practice 1 (page 79)

1. S 2. S 3. S 4. C 5. S 6. C 7. C 8. C 9. S 10. S

Practice 2 (page 80)

1. My brother is not too popular, but I like him. (1. c)
2. Many persons saw the attacker, but they refused to identify him. (2. b)
3. The people were ashamed of themselves, but they were too frightened. (3. c)
4. One of my friends saw the attack, but his mother would not let him testify. (4. a)
5. Today is the day of the picnic and the big game, but it's raining. (5. b)

Practice 3 (page 81)

1. I enjoy math, but I don't do well in it at school. (1. a)
2. My father is an FBI agent, and he is an expert decoder of cryptic messages. (2. b)
3. I enjoy watching television, but the commercials bother me. (3. c)
4. The show was funny, but we didn't like it. (4. c)
6. Vacations are my favorite times, and I make the most of them. (5. b)

Practice 4 (page 82)

(Sample Sentences)

1. My sister Jane is an excellent student, but my sister Mary does not do well in school.
2. Only three of my friends went to the party, for they were the only ones invited.
3. My brother is dating my best girlfriend, and my sister is dating my best friend's brother.
4. It became cloudy, and it started to rain.
5. She deserves the punishment, yet I feel sorry for her.

Practice 5 (page 83)

(Sample Sentences)

1. The test was hard, but I did very well on it.
2. The tall trees looked like soldiers standing at attention, and the flowers looked like pretty maidens dancing in the breeze.
3. John was outmatched in the set, but he won.
4. Sharon is going to the shore during school break, or she is going to the mountains.
5. Jennifer is a cheerful and happy person, and everyone likes her.

Practice 6 (page 84)

Sentences will vary.

Practice 7 (page 85)

(Sample Sentences)

1. I don't like the plan; therefore, I will not go along with you.
2. That doesn't sound too exciting; however, I may still go.
3. The class entered the auditorium and sat down; then the new instructor came in.
4. My parents don't like some of my friends; nevertheless, I invite them to my house.
5. Last year I received all A's; however, this year I'm failing two subjects.

Practice 8 (page 86)

(Sample Sentences)

1. We watered the plants; then we fertilized them.

Practice 8 (page 86) continued

2. All of my friends are champion ice skaters; however, not one of them wanted to enter the contest.

3. I prefer to stay out of politics; nevertheless, I was nominated to run for class president.

4. My campaign manager is excellent; therefore, I have a good chance of winning.

5. At the beginning, everyone promises to run a clean campaign; however, by the end, it usually becomes pretty muddy.

Practice 9 (page 87)

Sentences will vary.

Complex Sentences

Practice 1 (page 95)

1. X   2. C   3. S   4. X   5. S   6. S   7. X   8. X   9. C   10. X

1. After we went for a long walk in the park   4. that I am the youngest in my class

7. what he or she will be doing in the summer   8. when she grows up

10. Although she practices a lot

Practice 2 (page 96)

1. We had fun at the party, even though we hadn't wanted to go. (1. c)

2. We were frightened when we came home and found the windows and doors open. (2. a)

3. No one knew about the robberies because the victims were away on vacation. (3. b)

4. Seth is interested in sports, even if his best friend isn't. (4. c)

5. The entertainment during the intermission was not very good, until the comedians came on. (5. b)

Practice 3 (page 97)

1. The players were disappointed that they lost the game. (1. b)

2. It is amusing because it makes him look like a fool. (2. c)

3. Lots of people try hard, even though there is no chance for success. (3. b)

4. The animals in the zoo were not happy that the people were not feeding them. (4. b)

5. The students had mixed feelings about the teacher when he gave them the surprise exam. (5. a)

Practice 4 (page 98)

(Sample Sentences)

1. When the children were playing in the yard, they saw a huge bird.

2. Although my brother is a hard worker, he does not seem to be able to get ahead.

154

Practice 4 (page 98) continued

3. Even though I will not change my views about that topic, I will be elected class president.
4. He is well liked because he is always helpful, kind, and considerate.
5. The protesters were allowed to picket, even though no one agreed with their views.

Practice 5 (page 99)

(Sample Sentences)

1. Although I could definitely use the money, I will not earn it that way.
2. My friends are a lot of fun to be with, even though they kid me a lot.
3. We should try to do something now, even though help is on the way.
4. I will work very hard because you have so much faith in me.
5. As soon as we all got off the train, a crowd of people rushed toward us.

Practice 6 (page 100)

Sentences will vary.

Practice 7 (page 101)

Sentences will vary.

Practice 8 (page 102)

Sentences will vary.

Compound-Complex Sentences

Practice 1 (page 106)

1. X   2. CC   3. S   4. X   5. X   6. S   7. X   8. CC   9. X   10. C

Practice 2 (page 107)

1. The players were upset that they were losing, but they didn't give up. (1. c)
2. I believe that he has gone too far, and he will have to pay. (2. b)
3. My sister won a lot of prizes that she gave away, but she kept the biggest one. (3. c)
4. No one wanted the poor little cat except me, but my mother said that I couldn't keep it. (4. c)
5. The mysterious-looking man called my name, and then he slowly came toward me, but I was so frightened that I started to run. (5. b)

Practice 3 (page 108)

1. The truck was going so fast that it went out of control, and it crashed. (1. a)
2. Most people try different things because they like variety, but I don't. (2. c)
3. The home was antiseptically clean, and you could tell that no children had ever lived there. (3. a)
4. The escaped prisoner saw three police officers, and they had dogs with them that they used for tracking down escaped prisoners. (4. c)

Practice 3 (page 108) continued

5. The comedy was very funny, and we laughed so hard that our sides ached. (5. b)

Practice 4 (page 109)

(Sample Sentences)

1. We still had hope, even though the game was almost over, and our team had still not scored.
2. The coach called for a time-out because he wanted to talk to the players, and he wanted to build up their confidence.
3. The coach didn't yell at the team, and he didn't criticize them either, but he did give the players some sound advice because that's what they needed.
4. When the players went back on the field, they looked refreshed, and they looked stronger.
5. When the play was called, our team was ready, and they made the point.

Practice 5 (page 110)

(Sample Sentences)

1. I'm trying to be a neater person, but it's very difficult because my stuff seems to be all over the place.
2. My friends are constantly asking me to come play, but I cannot go outside because I need to finish cleaning my room.
3. I need to make an effort to be neat, but I haven't been able to because I start to think about other things I would rather do.
4. Even though my best friend is very busy, she always cleans up after herself because she is very neat, and she likes things in their proper place.
5. Even though the characters in some television shows seem busy all the time, they never seem to make a big mess, and they are always neat and organized.

Practice 6 (page 111)

Sentences will vary.

Sentence Expansion Using Modifiers

Practice 1 (page 116)

(Sample Answers)

1. pretty, smiling; enthusiastically
2. badly hurt; quickly
3. best; rapidly
4. big black; loudly
5. Sweet; pleasantly
6. mysterious old; dark green; light green; hysterically
7. little old; handsome young; quickly; crooked

Practice 2 (page 117)

(Sample Sentences)

1. The little white cat drinks cold milk slowly.
2. The losing team lost the last basketball game very badly.
3. I quickly read the sleepy child a funny story.
4. Hard-working John quickly answered the ringing phone.
5. Jerry cheerfully told pretty Jennifer the good news.

Combining Sentences

Practice 1 (page 126)

(Sample Sentences)

1. Jonathan is funny, and he likes to laugh a lot.
2. Alisa and Julie want to be cheerleaders.
3. Every morning Jeff, Lisa, and Kim ride their bikes to school.
4. Lee, Anna, and Terry are trying out for a part in the play, but Jason and Rachel are not trying out for a part in the play.
5. The story is a horror tale that frightens me and gives me nightmares.

Practice 2 (page 127)

(Sample Sentences)

1. Mary, Dave, and Sondra are happy.
2. Jakeel is good in sports, but his brother is not.
3. My friend's father is an engineer, his mother is a scientist, and his brother is a forest ranger.
4. Benita started to work on her paper, but she got tired, so she went to sleep.
5. My soft, small white cat, whose name is Feather, will only drink out of her own dish.

Practice 3 (page 128)

(Sample Sentences)

1. My sister, who is captain of the basketball team, is very tall and athletic. (complex)
   My tall, athletic sister is captain of the basketball team. (simple)
2. Gary loves to go horseback riding, but he shouldn't go because he's allergic to horses and sneezes a lot. (compound-complex)
   Gary sneezes a lot because he loves to go horseback riding, even though he is allergic to horses and shouldn't go. (complex)
3. The farmers were angry because wild dogs were eating their chickens, so they called a meeting and decided to hunt down the wild dogs. (compound-complex)
   The farmers were angry because wild dogs were eating their chickens; therefore, they called a meeting, and they decided to hunt down the wild dogs. (compound-complex)

Practice 3 (page 128) continued

The angry farmers called a meeting and decided to hunt down the wild dogs because the wild dogs were eating their chickens. (complex)

Practice 4 (page 129)

(Sample Sentences)

1. Even though Jennifer doesn't need the money, she baby-sits because she loves children. (complex)
   Jennifer loves children; therefore, she baby-sits, even though she doesn't need the money. (compound-complex)
2. The boy who is running keeps looking over his shoulder because the people are running after him, and they look angry. (compound-complex)
   The running boy keeps looking over his shoulder because the people running after him look angry. (complex)
3. Tomorrow is the championship game, but our star player is ill, so we are trying to postpone the game, but we can't. (compound)
   Since tomorrow is the championship game, and our star player is ill, we are trying to postpone the game, but we can't. (compound-complex)

Practice 5 (page 130)

(Sample Sentences)

1. The pretty young girl goes into the store.
2. My garden is filled with a variety of flowers, such as roses, lilies of the valley, and daisies.
3. A man wearing a dark suit and carrying a briefcase is walking slowly down the street.
   A man who is wearing a dark suit and carrying a briefcase is walking slowly down the street.
4. A limping sailor with a patch over one eye is walking quickly toward the diner.
   A sailor who has a patch over one eye and is limping is walking quickly toward the diner.
5. After a whistle blew, people started to come out of their houses to see what was happening.
6. When the frightened middle-aged man, who is carrying a package, sees two men are following him, he starts to run.

Posttest for Writing and Thinking Skills

Capitalization and Punctuation (page 132)

1. Dr. D. Chow asked whether we could meet at 5:00 p.m.
2. My mother said I could invite my friends to my Halloween party in October.
3. We will move from Stuart Rd. to Hardy Ave. on June 5, 2001.

Capitalization and Punctuation (page 132) continued

4. Lee is going to visit Mr. and Mrs. Jones on January 5, 2001.
5. Who is going to Leslie's party on Sunday?

Punctuation (page 132)

1. Kristin asked whether the story was funny.
2. Look out!
3. Who yelled so loudly?
4. Rodriguez did very well on the test.
5. Is Ally your best friend?

Direct Quotations (page 133)

1. Rueben asked, "Why are you so upset?"
2. Stacy said, "I need more time to finish all that homework."
3. Esteban said, "There is not enough time to do everything."
4. Mohammed asked, "What can I do to help?"
5. Sara said, "Speak to the teacher."

Direct and Indirect Quotations (page 133)

1. The twins said, "We want to go rollerblading."
2. We told them, "We have to do homework."
3. Rasheed said, "I can go after I practice the piano."
4. Molly said, "I have dance class after school."
5. Lee said, "I have to play soccer after school."

Contractions (page 133)

1. there's 2. he's 3. they'll 4. it's 5. let's 6. who's 7. where's 8. what's
9. won't 10. hasn't

Commas (page 134)

1. Sara's pretty red shoes look good on her feet. (NC)
2. That is a large scary-looking dog. (NC)
3. What beautiful long hair you have. (NC)
4. I cannot eat that hot, spicy food.
5. My itchy, sore arm hurts.

Recognizing Sentences (page 134)

1. There should be a line under numbers 1 and 4.

Word Order in Sentences (page 134)

1. A stitch in time saves nine.
2. There is no use crying over spilled milk.
3. Don't count your chickens before they hatch.
4. Flowers, such as roses, tulips, and daisies, are pretty.
5. Molly, Mike, and Jill are best friends, but they don't do everything together.

Combining Sentences (page 135)

1. Everywhere I go people give me unhealthy food to eat, but I want to stay healthy.
2. My friends say that they're cutting down on eating fatty foods, but every night they seem to eat fries and hot dogs.
3. I need to start eating less fatty foods, because I want to be a healthier person.
4. I am doing more exercises, and it's paying off.
5. My friends know what they should eat, but they still eat lots of junk food.

Shortening Sentences (page 136)

1. Marisa, Fred, and Molly like to run every day.
2. Kelly loves to eat Chinese, Mexican, Italian, and French food.
3. Roberto, Peggy, Kaitlin, and Kathy are all good friends.
4. We are going to a movie, a museum, and a party tomorrow.
5. Julie, Florenzio, Rashmid, Corrie, and Lee are playing soccer today.

Independent and Dependent Clauses (page 137)

1. Kristin is doing very well <u>because she is a hard worker</u>.
2. <u>When Molly is tired,</u> she stops working.
3. I eat ice cream, <u>even though it is cold outside</u>.
4. The doctor put Tracy in the hospital <u>when she had a very high fever</u>.
5. Bill got a stomachache <u>because he ate too much</u>.

Combining Independent and Dependent Clauses (page 137)

1. My friends go rollerblading every Friday because it is fun.
2. We refused to go indoors, even though it was snowing. **or** Even though it was snowing, we refused to go indoors.
3. They can get the supplies they need when they go shopping. **or** If they go shopping, they can get the supplies they need.
4. Two of my friends walked into a tree because they weren't looking where they were going.
5. Perez did very well on his exams because he does his homework every day.

Adjectives and Adverbs (page 138)

1. The silly clown ran faster than the children.
2. The best poem was read beautifully by Jacob.
3. Molly plays chess better than her brother, but he plays checkers the best of everyone.
4. The impatient children quickly ran outside.
5. My best friend always arrives at parties the earliest.

160